GROUNDWORK

of the

METAPHYSIC *of* MORALS

IMMANUEL KANT

GROUNDWORK

of the

METAPHYSIC *of* MORALS

Translated and analysed by
H. J. PATON

HARPER TORCHBOOKS / The Academy Library
Harper & Row, Publishers, New York
Grand Rapids, Philadelphia, St. Louis, San Francisco
London, Singapore, Sydney, Tokyo, Toronto

GROUNDWORK OF THE METAPHYSIC OF MORALS

Printed in the United States of America. This book was originally published under the title *The Moral Law* in the Philosophy series of the Hutchinson University Library, edited by Professor H. J. Paton, in 1948, with a second edition in 1953, and a third edition in 1956. It is here reprinted by arrangement with Hutchinson & Co., Ltd., London.

First HARPER TORCHBOOK edition published 1964 by
Harper & Row, Publishers, Incorporated
10 East 53rd Street
New York, N.Y. 10022

ISBN: 0-06-131159-6

94 95 MPC 40 39 38 37

CONTENTS

TRANSLATOR'S PREFACE

In spite of its horrifying title Kant's *Groundwork of the Metaphysic of Morals* is one of the small books which are truly great: it has exercised on human thought an influence almost ludicrously disproportionate to its size. In moral philosophy it ranks with the *Republic* of Plato and the *Ethics* of Aristotle; and perhaps—partly no doubt through the spread of Christian ideals and through the long experience of the human race during the last two thousand years—it shows in some respects a deeper insight even than these. Its main topic—the supreme principle of morality—is of the utmost importance to all who are not indifferent to the struggle of good against evil. Written, as it was, towards the end of the eighteenth century, it is couched in terms other than those that would be used to-day; but its message was never more needed than it is at present, when a somewhat arid empiricism is the prevailing fashion in philosophy. An exclusively empirical philosophy, as Kant himself argues, can have nothing to say about morality: it can only encourage us to be guided by our emotions, or at the best by an enlightened self-love, at the very time when the abyss between unregulated impulse or undiluted self-interest and moral principles has been so tragically displayed in practice. In the face of all this Kant offers us a defence of reasonableness in action: he reminds us that, however much the applications of morality may vary with varying circumstances, a good man is one who acts on the supposition that there is an unconditioned and objective moral standard holding for all men in virtue of their rationality as human beings. His claim to establish this is worth the serious consideration of all who are not content to regard themselves as victims of instinctive movements over which they have no intelligent control. Even if they do not agree with his doctrine, there is no doubt that they will see more in it the more they study it.

Unfortunately most readers in this country—and I fear even many teachers of philosophy—feel insufficiently at home in German to read this work most easily in the original. Kant has on the whole not been so fortunate in his translators as Hegel, and his English students may easily get the impression that he was a fumbler. He is very far indeed from being a fumbler, though he does expect too much from his readers: for example, he expects them to recognize at once in his long sentences the particular noun to which his excessive number of pronouns refer. I have kept in the main the structure of his sentences, which are, as it were, hewn out of the rock, but I have made no attempt to give a word for word translation. Every translation must to some extent be a veil, but it need not be an unbecoming one. I have striven to make his thought move in an English dress with some ease and even—if it were possible—with some elegance. Contrary to the usual opinion, what has struck me most in the course of my undertaking is how well he can write. And it is my hope that through this English rendering there may loom at least something of his liveliness of mind, his suppressed intellectual excitement, his moral earnestness, his pleasure in words, and even, it may be, something of his peculiar brand of humour, which is so dry that it might have come directly out of Scotland itself.

I have prefaced my translation by an analysis of the argument, and I have also added some notes. All this, I hope, may be of help to the inexperienced reader beginning the study of moral philosophy, and I trust that those who are more advanced will forgive me if at times I appear to underline the obvious. For more serious difficulties connected with the Critical Philosophy as a whole, I must refer readers to my commentary, *The Categorical Imperative*, and also—on the purely theoretical side of Kant's philosophy—to *Kant's Metaphysic of Experience*.

For ease of reference and in order to facilitate grasp of the structure of the argument I have inserted into the text some cross-headings. These, in distinction from Kant's own headings, are contained in square brackets. It should also be noted that Kant's own parentheses are in brackets. Passages between dashes have been made parentheses by me in order to make the main line of the argument easier to follow.

In the margin the numbers from i to xiv and from 1 to 128 give the pages of the *second* edition, which is the best published in Kant's lifetime, and I use these everywhere in my references. Unfortunately I did not use them in *The Categorical Imperative*, and, as they are not yet commonly accessible (though they ought to be), I have also given in the margin the pages of the edition issued by the Royal Prussian Academy in Berlin. The numbering of these pages begins with 387 so that there is no danger of confusion.

The only abbreviations I have used are *T.C.I.* and *K.M.E.* for my two books on Kant already mentioned.

I must in conclusion express my thanks to the many friends and pupils whom I have bothered on small points of translation, but especially to Dr. H. W. Cassirer for assuring me that my version is—or at least was—free from howlers; to Mr. W. H. Walsh for reading the proofs; and to Miss M. J. Levett, whose fierce sense of English usage has saved me from some of the Teutonisms into which a translator from the German can so easily fall. Above all I must thank my wife for typing the whole of my manuscript in these difficult days by an almost super-human effort which must surely have been inspired by the motive of duty for duty's sake.

H. J. Paton.

Corpus Christi College,
        Oxford.
August, 1947.

For some of the changes made in later editions I am indebted to criticisms from Principal T. M. Knox, Professor C. C. J. Webb, Dr. Dieter Henrich, and Mr. J. Kemp. I would add that the second and later editions of *The Categorical Imperative* give page references to the second German edition of Kant's work and so can be used more easily with the present translation.

H.J.P.

October, 1958.

ANALYSIS

OF THE

ARGUMENT

ANALYSIS OF THE ARGUMENT

PREFACE

Pages i–iii.—*The different branches of philosophy.*

THE three main branches of philosophy are logic, physics, and ethics. Of these *logic* is formal: it abstracts from all differences in the objects (or matter) about which we think and considers only the necessary laws (or forms) of thinking as such. Since it borrows nothing from our sensuous experience of objects, it must be regarded as a wholly non-empirical or *a priori* science. *Physics* deals with the laws of nature, and *ethics* with the laws of free moral action. These two philosophical sciences deal therefore with objects of thought which are sharply distinguished from one another.

Unlike logic, both physics and ethics must have an *empirical* part (one based on sensuous experience) as well as a non-empirical or *a priori* part (one not so based); for physical laws must apply to nature as an object of experience, and ethical laws must apply to human wills as affected by desires and instincts which can be known only by experience.

A philosopher of to-day would have to argue that these sciences have an *a priori* part rather than that they have an empirical part; and indeed many philosophers would deny the first possibility altogether. Nevertheless, if we take physics in a wide sense as the philosophy of nature, it appears to proceed in accordance with certain principles which are more than mere generalizations based on such data as are given to our senses. The task of formulating and, if possible, justifying these principles Kant regards as the *a priori* or pure part of physics (or as *a metaphysic of nature*). Among these principles he includes, for example, the principle that every event must have a cause, and this can never be proved (though it may be confirmed) by experience. He holds that it states a condition without which experience of nature, and so physical science itself, would be impossible.

It should be obvious that from experience of what men in fact do we are unable to prove what they ought to do; for we must admit that they often do what they ought not to do—provided we allow that there is such a thing as a moral 'ought' or a moral duty. Hence if there are moral principles in accordance with which men ought to act, knowledge of these principles must be *a priori* knowledge: it cannot be based on sensuous experience. The *a priori* or pure part of ethics is concerned with the *formulation* and *justification* of moral principles—with such terms as 'ought', 'duty', 'good' and 'evil', 'right' and 'wrong'. This *a priori* part of ethics may be called *a metaphysic of morals* (though at other times 'justification'—as opposed to 'formulation'—is reserved by Kant for a *critique of practical reason*). For detailed knowledge of particular human duties we require experience of human nature (and indeed of many other things). This belongs to the empirical part of ethics and is called by Kant '*practical anthropology*', though his use of the term is not altogether clear.

Kant's doctrine of *a priori* knowledge rests mainly on the assumption that mind—or reason, as he calls it—functions actively in accordance with principles which it can know and understand. He holds that such rational principles can be manifested, not only in thinking as such (which is studied in logic), but also in scientific knowledge and in moral action. We can separate out these rational principles, and we can understand how they are necessary for any rational being so far as he seeks to think rationally about the world and to act rationally in the world. If we believe that reason has no activity and no principles of its own and that mind is merely a bundle of sensations and desires, there can be for us no *a priori* knowledge; but we are hardly entitled to assert this without considering the arguments on the other side.

Pages iii–ix.—*The need for pure ethics.*

If the distinction between *a priori* and empirical ethics is sound, it is desirable to treat each part separately. The result of mixing them up is bound to be intellectual confusion, but it is also likely to lead to moral degeneration. If actions are to be morally good, they must be done for the sake of duty, and only the *a priori* or pure part of ethics can show us what the nature of duty is. By mixing up the different parts of ethics we may easily begin to confuse duty with self-interest, and this is bound to have disastrous effects in practice.

Pages ix–xi.—*The philosophy of willing as such*.

The *a priori* part of ethics is not to be confused with a philosophy of willing *as such*, since it deals, not with all willing, but with a particular *kind* of willing—namely, with willing that is morally good.

Pages xi–xiii.—*The aim of the* Groundwork.

The aim of the *Groundwork* is not to give us a complete exposition of the *a priori* part of ethics—that is, a complete metaphysic of morals. Its aim is rather to lay the *foundations* for such a metaphysic of morals, and so to separate out the really difficult part. Even as regards these foundations the *Groundwork* does not pretend to be complete: we require a full 'critique of practical reason' for this purpose. The need for such a critique of reason is, however, less pressing in practical matters than in theoretical, since ordinary human reason is a far safer guide in morals than it is in speculation; and Kant is anxious to avoid the complications of a full critique.

The essential point in all this is that the *Groundwork* has the limited, and yet all-important, aim of establishing the *supreme principle of morality*. It excludes all questions concerned with the *application* of this principle (although it occasionally gives illustrations of the way in which such applications may be made). Hence we should not expect from this book any detailed account of the application of moral principles, nor should we blame Kant for failing to supply it—still less should we invent theories of what he must have thought on this subject. If we want to know how he applied his supreme principle, we must read his neglected *Metaphysic of Morals*. In the *Groundwork* itself the only question to be considered is whether Kant has succeeded or failed in establishing the supreme principle of morality.

Page xiv.—*The method of the* Groundwork.

Kant's method is to start with the provisional assumption that our ordinary moral judgements may legitimately claim to be true. He then asks what are the *conditions* which must hold if these claims are to be justified. This is what he calls an *analytic* (or regressive) argument, and by it he hopes to discover a series of conditions till he comes to the ultimate condition of all moral judgements— the supreme principle of morality. He attempts to do this in Chapters I and II. In Chapter III his method is different. There he starts with the insight of reason into its own activity and attempts to derive from this the supreme principle of morality. This is what he calls a *synthetic* (or progressive) argument. If it were successful, we could reverse the direction of the argument in the first two chapters: beginning with the insight of reason into the principle of its own activity we could pass to the supreme principle of morality and from this to the ordinary moral judgements with which we started. In this way we should be able to justify our provisional assumption that ordinary moral judgements may legitimately claim to be true.

Chapter I attempts to lead us by an analytic argument from ordinary moral judgement to a philosophical statement of the first principle of morality. Chapter II, after dismissing the confusions of a 'popular' philosophy which works with examples and mixes the empirical with the *a priori*, proceeds (still by an analytic argument) to *formulate* the first principle of morality in different ways: it belongs to a metaphysic of morals. Chapter III attempts (in a synthetic argument) to *justify* the first principle of morality by deriving it from its source in pure practical reason: it belongs to a critique of pure practical reason.

ANALYSIS OF THE ARGUMENT

CHAPTER I

THE APPROACH TO MORAL PHILOSOPHY

Pages 1-3.—*The good will.*

THE only thing that is good without qualification or restriction is a good will. That is to say, a good will alone is good *in all circumstances* and in that sense is an absolute or unconditioned good. We may also describe it as the only thing that is good *in itself*, good independently of its relation to other things.

This does not mean that a good will is the only good. On the contrary, there are plenty of things which are good in many respects. These, however, are not good in all circumstances, and they may all be thoroughly bad when they are used by a bad will. They are therefore only conditioned goods—that is, good under certain conditions, not good absolutely or in themselves.

Pages 3-4.—*The good will and its results.*

The goodness of a good will is not derived from the goodness of the results which it produces. The conditioned goodness of its products cannot be the source of the unconditioned goodness which belongs to a good will alone. Besides, a good will continues to have its own unique goodness even where, by some misfortune, it is unable to produce the results at which it aims.

There is nothing in this to suggest that for Kant a good will does not aim at producing results. He holds, on the contrary, that a good will, and indeed any kind of will, must aim at producing results.

Pages 4-8.—*The function of reason.*

Ordinary moral consciousness supports the view that a good will alone is an unconditioned good. Indeed this is the presupposition (or condition) of all our ordinary moral judgements.

Nevertheless the claim may seem to be fantastic, and we must seek further corroboration by considering the function of reason in action.

In order to do this we have to presuppose that in organic life every organ has a purpose or function to which it is well adapted. This applies also to mental life; and in human beings reason is, as it were, the organ which controls action, just as instinct is the organ which controls action in animals. If the function of reason in action were merely to attain happiness, this is a purpose for which instinct would have been a very much better guide. Hence if we assume that reason, like other organs, must be well adapted to its purpose, its purpose cannot be merely to produce a will which is good as a means to happiness, but rather to produce a will which is good in itself.

Such a purposive (or teleological) view of nature is not readily accepted to-day. We need only note that Kant does hold this belief (though by no means in a simple form) and that it is very much more fundamental to his ethics than is commonly supposed. In particular we should note that reason in action has for him two main functions, the first of which has to be subordinated to the second. The first function is to secure the individual's own happiness (a conditioned good), while the second is to manifest a will good in itself (an unconditioned good).

Page 8.—*The good will and duty.*

Under human conditions, where we have to struggle against unruly impulses and desires, a good will is manifested in acting *for the sake of duty*. Hence if we are to understand human goodness, we must examine the concept of duty. Human goodness is most conspicuous in struggling against the obstacles placed in its way by unruly impulses, but it must not be thought that goodness as such consists in overcoming obstacles. On the contrary, a perfectly good will would have no obstacles to overcome, and the concept of duty (which involves the overcoming of obstacles) would not apply to such a perfect will.

Pages 8-13.—*The motive of duty.*

A human action is morally good, not because it is done from immediate inclination—still less because it is done from self-interest—but because it is done for the sake of duty. This is Kant's first proposition about duty, though he does not state it in this general form.

An action—even if it accords with duty and is in that sense right—is not commonly regarded as morally good if it is done solely out of self-interest. We may, however, be inclined to attribute moral goodness to right actions done solely from some immediate inclination—for example, from a direct impulse of sympathy or generosity. In order to test this we must *isolate* our motives: we must consider first an action done solely out of inclination and *not* out of duty, and then an action done solely out of duty and *not* out of inclination. If we do this, then, we shall find—to take the case most favourable to immediate inclination—that an action done solely out of natural sympathy may be right and praiseworthy, but that nevertheless it has no distinctively moral worth. The same kind of action done solely out of duty does have distinctively moral worth. The goodness shown in helping others is all the more conspicuous if a man does this for the sake of duty at a time when he is fully occupied with his own troubles and when he is not impelled to do so by his natural inclinations.

Kant's doctrine would be absurd if it meant that the presence of a natural inclination to good actions (or even of a feeling of satisfaction in doing them) detracted from their moral worth. The ambiguity of his language lends some colour to this interpretation, which is almost universally accepted. Thus he says that a man shows moral worth if he does good, not from inclination, but from duty. But we must remember that he is here contrasting two motives taken in *isolation* in order to find out which of them is the source of moral worth. He would have avoided the ambiguity if he had said that a man shows moral worth, not in doing good from inclination, but in doing it for the sake of duty. It is the motive of duty, not the motive of inclination, that gives moral worth to an action.

Whether these two kinds of motive can be present in the same moral action and whether one can support the other is a question which is not even raised in this passage nor is it discussed at all in the *Groundwork*. Kant's assumption on this subject is that if an action is to be morally good, the motive of duty, while it may be present *at the same time* as other motives, must by itself be sufficient to determine the action. Furthermore, he never wavers in the belief that generous inclinations are a help in doing good actions, that for this reason it is a duty to cultivate them, and that without them a great moral adornment would be absent from the world.

It should also be observed that, so far from decrying happiness, Kant holds that we have at least an indirect duty to seek our own happiness.

Pages 13-14.—*The formal principle of duty.*

Kant's second proposition is this: *An action done from duty has its moral worth, not from the results it attains or seeks to attain, but from a formal principle or maxim—the principle of doing one's duty whatever that duty may be.*

This re-states the first proposition in a more technical way. We have already seen that a good will cannot derive its unconditioned goodness from the conditioned goodness of the *results* at which it aims, and this is true also of the morally good actions in which a good will acting for the sake of duty is manifested. What we have to do now is to state our doctrine in terms of what Kant calls 'maxims'.

A maxim is a principle upon which we act. It is a purely personal principle—not a copy-book maxim—and it may be good or it may be bad. Kant calls it a 'subjective' principle, meaning by this a principle on which a rational agent (or subject of action) *does* act—a principle manifested in actions which are in fact performed. An 'objective' principle, on the other hand, is one on which every rational agent *would necessarily* act if reason had full control over his actions, and therefore one on which he *ought* to act if he is so irrational as to be tempted to act otherwise. Only when we act on objective principles do they become *also* subjective, but they continue to be objective whether we act on them or not.

We need not formulate in words the maxim of our action, but if we know what we are doing and will our action as an action of a particular *kind*, then our action has a maxim or subjective principle. A maxim is thus always some sort of *general* principle under which we will a particular action. Thus if I decide to commit suicide in order to avoid unhappiness, I may be said to act on the principle or maxim 'I will kill myself *whenever* life offers more pain than pleasure'.

All such maxims are *material* maxims: they generalize a particular action with its particular motive and its intended result. Since the moral goodness of an action cannot be derived from its intended results, it manifestly cannot be derived from a material maxim of this kind.

The maxim which gives moral worth to actions is the maxim or principle of doing one's duty whatever one's duty may be. Such a maxim is empty of any particular matter: it is not a maxim of satisfying particular desires or attaining particular results. In Kant's language it is a *formal* maxim. To act for the sake of duty is to act on a formal maxim 'irrespective of all objects of the faculty of desire'. A good man adopts or rejects the material maxim of any proposed action according as it harmonizes or conflicts with the controlling and formal maxim of doing his duty for its own sake. Only such 'dutiful' actions can be morally good.

Pages 14–17.—*Reverence for the law*.

A third proposition is alleged to follow from the first two. It is this: *Duty is the necessity to act out of reverence for the law.*

This proposition cannot be derived from the first two unless we can read into them a good deal more than has been explicitly stated: both 'reverence' and 'the law' appear to be terms which we have not met in the premises. Furthermore the proposition itself is not altogether clear. Perhaps it would be better to say that to act on the maxim of doing one's duty for its own sake is to act out of reverence for the law.

It is not altogether easy to follow Kant's argument. He appears to hold that if the maxim of a morally good action is a *formal* maxim (not a material maxim of satisfying one's desires), it must be a maxim of acting reasonably—that is, of acting on a law valid for all rational beings as such independently of their particular desires. Because of our human frailty such a law must appear to us as a law of duty, a law which commands or compels obedience. Such a law, considered as *imposed* upon us, must excite a feeling analogous to fear. Considered, on the other hand, as self-imposed (since it is imposed by our own rational nature), it must excite a feeling analogous to inclination or attraction. This complex feeling is *reverence* (or respect)—a unique feeling which is due, not to any stimulus of the senses, but to the thought that my will is subordinated to such a universal law independently of any influence of sense. So far as the motive of a good action is to be found in feeling, we must say that a morally good action is one which is done out of reverence for the law, and that this is what gives it its unique and unconditioned value.

Pages 17-20.—*The categorical imperative.*

It may seem to be a very strange kind of law which the good man is supposed to reverence and obey. It is a law which does not depend on our desire for particular consequences and does not in itself even prescribe any particular actions: all it imposes on us is law-abidingness for its own sake—'the conformity of actions to universal law as such'. To many this conception must seem empty, if not revolting, and we have certainly passed from ordinary moral judgements to the very highest pitch of philosophical abstraction—to the *form* common to all genuine morality, whatever its matter may be. Yet is not Kant merely saying the minimum that can and must be said about morality? A man is morally good, not as seeking to satisfy his own desires or to attain his own happiness (though he may do both these things), but as seeking to obey a law valid for *all* men and to follow an objective standard not determined by his own desires.

Because of the obstacles due to our impulses and desires, this law appears to us as a law that we *ought* to obey for its own sake, and so as what Kant calls a categorical imperative. We are here given the first statement of the categorical imperative (though in a negative form): 'I ought never to act except in such a way *that I can also will that my maxim should become a universal law*'. This is the first formulation of the supreme principle of morality—the ultimate condition of all particular moral laws and all ordinary moral judgements. From this all moral laws must be '*derived*'—in the sense that it is 'original', while they are 'derivative' or dependent. Yet, as the formula itself shows, there is no question of *deducing* particular moral laws from the empty form of law as such. On the contrary, what we have to do is to examine the *material* maxims of our contemplated actions and to accept or reject them according as they can or cannot be willed as universal laws—that is, as laws valid for all men, and not as special privileges of our own.

From the example Kant gives in applying this method to the contemplated action of telling a lie it is obvious that he believed the application of his principle to be easier than it in fact is. Nevertheless he has stated the supreme condition of moral action, and his sharp distinction be:ween moral action and merely prudential or impulsive action is fundamentally sound.

Pages 20–22.—*Ordinary practical reason.*

The ordinary good man does not formulate this moral principle in abstraction, but he does use this principle in making particular moral judgements. Indeed in practical affairs (though not in speculation) ordinary human reason is almost a better guide than philosophy. Might it not then be advisable to leave moral questions to the ordinary man and to regard moral philosophy as the occupation (or the game) of the philosophical specialist?

Pages 22–24.—*The need for philosophy.*

The ordinary man needs philosophy because the claims of pleasure tempt him to become a self-deceiver and to argue sophistically against what appear to be the harsh demands of morality. This gives rise to what Kant calls a natural *dialectic*—a tendency to indulge in plausible arguments which contradict one another, and in this way to undermine the claims of duty. This may be disastrous to morality in practice, so disastrous that in the end ordinary human reason is impelled to seek for some solution of its difficulties. This solution is to be found only in philosophy, and in particular in a critique of practical reason, which will trace our moral principle to its source in reason itself.

ANALYSIS OF THE ARGUMENT

CHAPTER II

OUTLINE OF A METAPHYSIC OF MORALS

Pages 25-30.—*The use of examples.*

ALTHOUGH we have extracted the supreme principle of morality from ordinary moral judgements, this does not mean that we have arrived at it by generalizing from examples of morally good actions given to us in experience. Such an empirical method would be characteristic of a 'popular' philosophy, which depends on examples and illustrations. In actual fact we can never be sure that there are any examples of 'dutiful' actions (actions whose determining motive is that of duty). What we are discussing is not what men in fact do, but what they ought to do.

Even if we had experience of dutiful actions, this would not be enough for our purposes. What we have to show is that there is a moral law valid for all rational beings as such and for all men in virtue of their rationality—a law which rational beings as such ought to follow if they are tempted to do otherwise. This could never be established by any experience of actual human behaviour.

Furthermore, examples of morally good action can never be a substitute for moral principles nor can they supply a ground on which moral principles can be based. It is only if we already possess moral principles that we can judge an action to be an example of moral goodness.

Morality is not a matter of blind imitation, and the most that examples can do is to encourage us to do our duty: they can show that right action is possible, and they can bring it more vividly before our minds.

Pages 30-34.—*Popular philosophy.*

Popular philosophy, instead of separating sharply the *a priori* and empirical parts of ethics, offers us a disgusting hotch-potch in which *a priori* and empirical elements are hopelessly intermingled. Moral principles are confused with principles of self-interest, and this has the effect of weakening the claims of morality in a misguided effort to strengthen them.

Pages 34–36.—*Review of conclusions.*

Moral principles must be grasped entirely *a priori*. To mix them up with empirical considerations of self-interest and the like is not merely a confusion of thought but an obstacle in the way of moral progress. Hence before we attempt to apply moral principles we must endeavour to formulate them precisely in a pure metaphysic of morals from which empirical considerations are excluded.

Pages 36–39.—*Imperatives in general.*

We must now try to explain what is meant by words like 'good' and 'ought', and in particular what is meant by an 'imperative'. There are different kinds of imperative, but we have to deal first with imperatives *in general* (or what is common to all kinds of imperative): we are not concerned merely with the moral imperative (though we may have this particularly in mind). This is a source of difficulty on a first reading, especially as the word 'good' has different senses when used in connection with different kinds of imperative.

We begin with the conception of a rational agent. A rational agent is one who has the power to act in accordance with his idea of laws—that is, to act in accordance with *principles*. This is what we mean when we say that he has a *will*. 'Practical reason' is another term for such a will.

We have already seen that the actions of rational agents have a *subjective* principle or maxim, and that in beings who are only imperfectly rational such subjective principles must be distinguished from *objective* principles—that is, from principles on which a rational agent would necessarily act if reason had full control over passion. So far as an agent acts on objective principles, his will and his actions may be described as *in some sense* 'good'.

Imperfectly rational beings like men do not always act on objective principles: they may do so or they may not. This is expressed more technically by saying that for men actions which are objectively necessary are subjectively contingent.

To imperfectly rational beings objective principles seem almost to *constrain* or (in Kant's technical language) to *necessitate* the will —that is, they seem to be imposed upon the will from without instead of being its *necessary* manifestation (as they would be in the case of a wholly rational agent). There is in this respect a sharp difference between being *necessary*, and being *necessitating*, for a rational will.

Where an objective principle is conceived as *necessitating* (and not merely as necessary), it may be described as a *command*. The formula of such a command may be called an *imperative* (though Kant does not in practice distinguish sharply between a command and an imperative).

All imperatives (not merely moral ones) are expressed by the words '*I ought*'. 'I ought' may be said to express from the side of the subject the relation of *necessitation* which holds between a principle recognized as objective and an imperfectly rational will. When I say that 'I ought' to do something, I mean that I recognize an action of this kind to be imposed or necessitated by an objective principle valid for any rational agent as such.

Since imperatives are objective principles considered as necessitating, and since action in accordance with objective principles is good action (in some sense), all imperatives command us to do *good* actions (not merely—as some philosophers hold—actions that are obligatory or right).

A perfectly rational and wholly good agent would *necessarily* act on the same objective principles which for us are imperatives, and so would manifest a kind of goodness just as we do when we obey these imperatives. But for him such objective principles would not be imperatives: they would be necessary but not necessitating, and the will which followed them could be described as a 'holy' will. Where we say 'I ought', an agent of this kind would say 'I will'. He would have no duties nor would he feel reverence for the moral law (but something more akin to love).

In an important footnote Kant explains, if somewhat obscurely, what he means by such terms as 'inclination' and 'interest', and he distinguishes between 'pathological' (or sensuous) interest and 'practical' (or moral) interest. For this *see* the analysis of pages 121–123.

Pages 39–44.—*Classification of imperatives*

There are three different kinds of imperatives. Since imperatives are objective principles considered as necessitating, there must equally be three corresponding kinds of objective principle and three corresponding kinds (or senses) of 'good'.

Some objective principles are *conditioned* by a will for some end—that is to say, they would necessarily be followed by a fully rational agent *if* he willed the end. These principles give rise to *hypothetical* imperatives, which have the general form '*If* I will this end, I ought to do such and such'. They bid us do actions which are *good as means* to an end that we already will (or might will).

When the end is merely one that we might will, the imperatives are *problematic* or *technical*. They may be called imperatives of skill, and the actions they enjoin are good in the sense of being '*skilful*' or '*useful*'.

Where the end is one that every rational agent wills by his very nature, the imperatives are *assertoric* or *pragmatic*. The end which every rational agent wills by his very nature is his own happiness, and the actions enjoined by a pragmatic imperative are good in the sense of being '*prudent*'.

Some objective principles are *unconditioned*: they would necessarily be followed by a fully rational agent but are not based on the previous willing of some further end. These principles give rise to *categorical* imperatives, which have the general form 'I ought to do such and such' (without any '*if*' as a prior condition). They may also be called 'apodeictic'—that is, necessary in the sense of being unconditioned and absolute. These are the unconditioned imperatives of morality, and the actions they enjoin are *morally good*—good in themselves and not merely good as a means to some further end.

The different kinds of imperative exercise a different kind of *necessitation*. This difference may be marked by describing them as *rules* of skill, *counsels* of prudence, *commands* (or *laws*) of morality. Only commands or laws are absolutely binding.

Pages 44-50.—*How are imperatives possible?*

We have now to consider how these imperatives are 'possible'—
that is, how they can be *justified*. To justify them is to show that
the principles on which they bid us act are *objective* in the sense
of being valid for any rational being as such. Kant always assumes
that a principle on which a fully rational agent as such would
necessarily act is also one on which an imperfectly rational agent
ought to act if he is tempted to do otherwise.

In order to understand the argument we must grasp the
distinction between analytic and synthetic propositions.

In an *analytic* proposition the predicate is contained in the subject-
concept and can be derived by analysis of the subject-concept.
Thus 'Every *effect* must have a cause' is an analytic proposition;
for it is impossible to conceive an effect without conceiving it as
having a cause. Hence in order to justify an analytic proposition
we do not need to go beyond the concept of the subject. In a
synthetic proposition the predicate is *not* contained in the subject-
concept and cannot be derived by analysis of the subject-concept.
Thus 'Every *event* must have a cause' is a synthetic proposition;
for it is possible to conceive an event without conceiving that it
has a cause. In order to justify any synthetic proposition we have
to go beyond the concept of the subject and discover some 'third
term' which will entitle us to attribute the predicate to the subject.

*Any fully rational agent who wills an end necessarily wills the
means to the end.* This is an analytic proposition; for to will (and
not merely to wish) an end is to will the action which is a means
to this end. Hence any rational agent who wills an end *ought* to
will the means to this end if he is irrational enough to be tempted
to do otherwise. There is thus no difficulty in justifying *imperatives
of skill*.

It should be noted that in finding out what are in fact the
means to our ends we make use of synthetic propositions: we
have to discover what causes will produce certain desired effects,
and it is impossible to discover the cause of any effect by a mere
analysis of the concept of the effect by itself. These synthetic
propositions, however, are theoretical only: when we know what
cause will produce the desired effect, the principle determining our
will as rational beings is the analytic proposition that any fully

rational agent who wills an end necessarily wills the known means to that end.

When we come to consider *imperatives of prudence*, we meet a special difficulty. Although happiness is an end which we all in fact seek, our concept of it is unfortunately vague and indeterminate: we do not know clearly what our end is. At times Kant himself speaks as if the pursuit of happiness were merely a search for the means to the maximum possible amount of pleasant feeling throughout the whole course of life. At other times he recognizes that it involves the choice and harmonizing of ends as well as of the means to them. Apart from these difficulties, however, imperatives of prudence are justified in the same way as imperatives or skill. They rest on the analytic proposition that any fully rational agent who wills an end must necessarily will the known means to that end.

This kind of justification is not possible in the case of *moral or categorical imperatives*; for when I recognize a moral duty by saying 'I ought to do such and such', this does not rest on the presupposition that some further end is already willed. To justify a categorical imperative we have to show that a fully rational agent would necessarily act in a certain way—not *if* he happens to want something else, but simply and solely as a rational agent. A predicate of this kind, however, is not contained in the concept 'rational agent' and cannot be derived by analysis of this concept. The proposition is not analytic but synthetic, and yet it is an assertion of what a rational agent as such would *necessarily* do. Such an assertion can never be justified by experience of examples nor, as we have seen, can we be sure that we have any such experience. The proposition is not merely synthetic, but also *a priori*, and the difficulty of justifying such a proposition is likely to be very great. This task must be postponed till later.

Pages 51-52.—*The Formula of Universal Law.*

Our first problem is to *formulate* the categorical imperative— that is, to state what it commands or enjoins. This topic is pursued ostensibly for its own sake, and we are given a succession of formulæ; but in all this the analytic argument to the supreme principle or morality (the principle of autonomy) is still being carried on;

and we shall find later that it is the principle of autonomy which
enables us to connect morality with the Idea of freedom as
expounded in the final chapter.

A categorical imperative, as we have already seen, merely bids
us act in accordance with universal law as such—that is, it bids us
act on a principle valid for all rational beings as such, and not
merely on one that is valid *if* we happen to want some further
end. Hence it bids us accept or reject the *material* maxim of a contemplated action according as it can or cannot be willed also as
a universal law. We may express this in the formula '*Act only on
that maxim through which you can at the same time will that it should
become a universal law*'.

There is thus only one categorical imperative. We may also
more loosely describe as categorical imperatives the various particular moral laws in which the one general categorical imperative
is applied—as, for example, the law 'Thou shalt not kill'. Such
laws are all 'derived' from the one categorical imperative as their
principle. In the *Groundwork* Kant appears to think that they can
be derived from this formula by itself, but in the *Critique of Practical
Reason* he holds that for this purpose we require to make use of
the formula which immediately follows.

Page 52.—*The Formula of the Law of Nature.*

'*Act as if the maxim of your action were to become through your
will a universal law of nature.*'

This formula, though subordinate to the previous one, is
entirely distinct from it: it refers to a law of nature, not of freedom,
and it is the formula which Kant himself uses in his illustrations.
He gives no explanation of why he does so beyond saying—on
page 81—that there is an *analogy* between the universal law of
morality and the universal law of nature. The subject is a highly
technical one and is expounded further in the *Critique of Practical
Reason*, but for this I must refer to my book, *The Categorical
Imperative*, especially pages 157–164.

A law of nature is primarily a law of cause and effect. Nevertheless, when Kant asks us to consider our maxims *as if* they were
laws of nature, he treats them as purposive (or teleological) laws.
He is already supposing that nature—or at least human nature—

is teleological or is what he later calls a kingdom of nature and not a mere mechanism.

In spite of these difficulties and complications Kant's doctrine is simple. He holds that a man is morally good, not so far as he acts from passion or self-interest, but so far as he acts on an impersonal principle valid for others as well as for himself. This is the *essence* of morality; but if we wish to *test* the maxim of a proposed action we must ask whether, if universally adopted, it would further a systematic harmony of purposes in the individual and in the human race. Only if it would do this can we say that it is fit to be willed as a universal moral law.

The *application* of such a test is manifestly impossible without empirical knowledge of human nature, and Kant takes this for granted in his illustrations.

Pages 52–57.—*Illustrations.*

Duties may be divided into duties towards self and duties towards others, and again into perfect and imperfect duties. This gives us four main *types* of duty, and Kant gives us one illustration of each type in order to show that his formula can be applied to all four.

A perfect duty is one which admits of no exception in the interests of inclination. Under this heading the examples given are the ban on suicide and on making a false promise in order to receive a loan. We are not entitled to commit suicide because we have a strong inclination to do so, nor are we entitled to pay our debt to one man and not to another because we happen to like him better. In the case of imperfect duties the position is different: we are bound only to adopt the *maxim* of developing our talents and of helping others, and we are to some extent entitled to decide arbitrarily *which* talents we will develop and *which* persons we will help. There is here a certain 'latitude' or 'playroom' for mere inclination.

In the case of duties towards self Kant assumes that our various capacities have a natural function or purpose in life. It is a perfect duty *not* to thwart such purposes; and it is also a positive, but imperfect, duty to further such purposes.

In the case of duties towards others we have a perfect duty

not to thwart the realization of a possible systematic harmony of purposes among men; and we have a positive, but imperfect, duty to further the realization of such a systematic harmony.

The qualifications to be attached to such principles are necessarily omitted in such a book as the *Groundwork*.

Pages 57–59.—*The canon of moral judgement.*

The general canon of moral judgement is that we should be able to *will* that the maxim of our action should become a universal law (of *freedom*). When we consider our maxims as possible (teleological) laws of *nature*, we find that some of them cannot even be *conceived* as such laws: for example, a law that self-love (which considered as falling under a law of nature becomes something like a feeling—or instinct—of self-preservation) should both further and destroy life is inconceivable. In such a case the maxim is opposed to perfect or strict duty. Other maxims, though not inconceivable as possible (teleological) laws of nature, yet cannot be consistently *willed* as such laws: there would be inconsistency or inconsequence in willing, for example, that men should possess talents, and yet should never use them. Maxims of this kind are opposed to imperfect duty.

Whatever may be thought of the details of Kant's argument— and the argument against suicide is particularly weak—we have to ask ourselves whether a teleological view of human nature is not necessary to ethics, just as some sort of teleological view of the human body is necessary to medicine. It should also be observed that on Kant's view moral questions are not merely questions of what we can *think* but of what we can *will*, and that bad action involves, not a theoretical contradiction, but an opposition (or antagonism) of inclination to a rational will supposed to be in some sense actually present in ourselves.

Pages 59–63.—*The need for pure ethics.*

Kant re-emphasizes his previous contentions on this subject.

Pages 63–67.—*The Formula of the End in Itself.*

Act in such a way that you always treat humanity, whether in your own person or in the person of any other, never simply as a means, but always at the same time as an end.

This formula brings in a second aspect of all action; for all rational action, besides having a principle, must also set before itself an end. Ends—like principles—may be merely *subjective*: they may be arbitrarily adopted by an individual. Subjective or relative ends which a particular agent seeks to produce are, as we have seen, the ground only of *hypothetical* imperatives, and their value is relative and conditioned. If there were also *objective* ends given to us by reason, ends which in all circumstances a fully rational agent would necessarily pursue, these would have an absolute and unconditioned value. They would also be ends which an imperfectly rational agent *ought* to pursue if he were irrational enough to be tempted to do otherwise.

Such ends could not be mere products of our actions, for—as we have seen all along—no mere product of our action can have an unconditioned and absolute value. They must be already existent ends; and their mere existence would impose on us the duty of pursuing them (so far as this was in our power). That is to say, they would be the *ground* of a *categorical* imperative in somewhat the same way as merely subjective ends are the ground of hypothetical imperatives. Such ends may be described as ends in themselves—not merely as ends relative to particular rational agents.

Only rational agents or *persons* can be ends in themselves. As they alone can have an unconditioned and absolute value, it is wrong to use them simply as means to an end whose value is only relative. Without such ends in themselves there would be no unconditioned good, no supreme principle of action, and so—for human beings—no categorical imperative. Thus, like our first formula, the Formula of the End in Itself follows from the very essence of the categorical imperative—provided we remember that all action must have an end as well as a principle.

Kant adds that every rational agent necessarily conceives his own existence in this way on grounds valid for every rational agent as such. The justification for this depends, however, on his account of the Idea of freedom, which is reserved till later.

The new formula, like the first one, must give rise to particular categorical imperatives when applied to the special nature or man.

Pages 67–68.—*Illustrations.*

The same set of examples brings out even more clearly the teleological presuppositions necessary for any *test* by which the categorical imperative can be applied. We have a perfect duty *not* to use ourselves or others *merely* as a means to the satisfaction of our inclinations. We have an imperfect, but *positive*, duty to further the ends of nature in ourselves and in others—that is, to seek our own perfection and the happiness of others.

As Kant himself indicates in one passage, we are concerned only with very general *types* of duty. It would be quite unfair to complain that he does not deal with all the qualifications that might be necessary in dealing with special problems.

Pages 69–71.—*The Formula of Autonomy.*

So act that your will can regard itself at the same time as making universal law through its maxim.

This formula may seem at first sight to be a mere repetition of the Formula of Universal Law. It has, however, the advantage of making explicit the doctrine that the categorical imperative bids us, not merely to follow universal law, but to follow a universal law which we ourselves make as rational agents and one which we ourselves particularize through our maxims. This is for Kant the most important formulation of the supreme principle of morality, since it leads straight to the Idea of freedom. We are subject to the moral law only because it is the necessary expression of our own nature as rational agents.

The Formula of Autonomy—though the argument is obscurely stated—is derived from combining the Formula of Universal Law and the Formula of the End in Itself. We have not only seen that we are bound to obey the law in virtue of its universality (its objective validity for all rational agents); we have also seen that rational agents as subjects are the *ground* of this categorical imperative. If this is so, the law which we are bound to obey must be the product of our own will (so far as we are rational agents)—that is to say, it rests on 'the Idea of the will of every rational being as a will which makes universal law'.

Kant puts his point more simply later—page 83—when he says of a rational being 'it is precisely the fitness of his maxims to make universal law that marks him out as an end in himself'. If a rational agent is truly an end in himself, he must be the author of the laws which he is bound to obey, and it is this which gives him his supreme value.

Pages 71–74.—*The exclusion of interest.*

A categorical imperative excludes interest: it says simply 'I ought to do this', and it does *not* say 'I ought to do this *if* I happen to want that'. This was implicit in our previous formulae from the mere fact that they were formulae of an imperative recognized to be categorical. It is now made explicit in the Formula of Autonomy. A will may be subject to laws because of some interest (as we have seen in hypothetical imperatives). A will which is not subject to law because of any interest can be subject only to laws which it itself makes. Only if we conceive the will as making its own laws can we understand how an imperative can exclude interest and so be categorical. The supreme merit of the Formula of Autonomy is this: by the express statement that a rational will makes the laws which it is bound to obey the essential character of the categorical imperative is for the first time made fully explicit. Hence the Formula of Autonomy follows directly from the character of the categorical imperative itself.

All philosophies which seek to explain moral obligation by any kind of interest make a categorical imperative inconceivable and deny morality altogether. They may all be said to propound a doctrine of *heteronomy*—that is, they portray the will as bound only by a law which has its origin in some object or end *other* than the will itself. Theories of this kind can give rise only to hypothetical, and so non-moral, imperatives.

Pages 74–77.—*The Formula of the Kingdom of Ends.*

So act as if you were through your maxims a law-making member of a kingdom of ends.

This formula springs directly from the Formula of Autonomy. So far as rational agents are all subject to universal laws which they themselves make, they constitute a kingdom—that is, a State or commonwealth. So far as these laws bid them treat each other as ends in themselves, the kingdom so constituted is a kingdom of ends. These ends cover, not only persons as ends in themselves, but also the personal ends which each of these may set before himself in accordance with universal law. The concept of the kingdom of ends is connected with the Idea of an intelligible world in the final chapter.

We must distinguish between the *members* of such a kingdom (all finite rational agents) and its supreme *head* (an infinite rational agent). As law-making members of such a kingdom rational agents have what is called 'dignity'—that is, an intrinsic, unconditioned, incomparable worth or worthiness.

Pages 77–79.—*The dignity of virtue.*

A thing has a *price* if any substitute or equivalent can be found for it. It has *dignity* or worthiness if it admits of no equivalent.

Morality or virtue—and humanity so far as it is capable of morality—alone has dignity. In this respect it cannot be compared with things that have economic value (a market price) or even with things that have an æsthetic value (a fancy price). The incomparable worth of a good man springs from his being a law-making member in a kingdom of ends.

Pages 79–81.—*Review of the Formulae.*

In the final review three formulae only are mentioned: (1) the Formula of the Law of Nature, (2) the Formula of the End in Itself, and (3) the Formula of the Kingdom of Ends. The first formula is said to be concerned with the form of a moral maxim—that is, with its universality; the second with its matter—that is, with its ends; while the third combines both form and matter. In addition, however, the Formula of Universal Law is mentioned as the strict test to apply (presumably because it is concerned primarily with the motive of moral action). The purpose of the others is to bring the Idea of duty closer to intuition (or imagination).

A new version is given for the Formula of the Kingdom of Ends. '*All maxims as proceeding from our own making of laws ought to harmonize with a possible kingdom of ends as a kingdom of nature.*'

The kingdom of nature has not been mentioned before, and it seems to stand to the kingdom of ends in the same sort of relation as the universal law of nature stands to the universal law of freedom. Kant makes it perfectly clear that when he regards nature as offering an analogy for morality, nature is considered to be teleological.

The Formula of Autonomy is here amalgamated with the Formula of the Kingdom of Ends.

Pages 81–87.—*Review of the whole argument.*

The final review summarizes the whole argument from beginning to end—from the concept of a good will to the concept of the dignity of virtue and the dignity of man as capable of virtue. The transitions from one formula to another are simplified and in some ways improved. The most/notable addition is, however, the account given of the kingdom of nature. The kingdom of ends can be realized only if *all* men obey the categorical imperative, but even this would not be enough: unless nature itself also *co-operates* with our moral strivings, this ideal can never be attained. We cannot be confident of co-operation either from other men or from nature, but in spite of this the imperative which bids us act as law-making members of a kingdom of ends remains categorical. We ought to pursue this ideal whether or not we can expect to secure results, and this disinterested pursuit of the moral ideal is at once the source of man's dignity and the standard by which he must be judged.

Pages 87–88.—*Autonomy of the will.*

We have shown by an analytic argument that the principle of the autonomy of the will (and consequently also a categorical imperative enjoining action in accordance with such autonomy) is a necessary condition of the validity of moral judgements. If, however, we wish to establish the validity of the principle of autonomy, we must pass beyond our judgements about moral actions to a critique of pure practical reason.

Pages 88–89.—*Heteronomy of the will.*

Any moral philosophy which rejects the principle of autonomy has to fall back on a principle of heteronomy: it must make the

law governing human action depend, not on the will itself, but on
objects other than the will. Such a view can give rise only to
hypothetical and so non-moral imperatives.

Pages 89–90.—*Classification of heteronomous principles.*

Heteronomous principles are either *empirical* or *rational*. Whei.
they are empirical, their principle is always the pursuit of *happiness*,
although some of them may be based on natural feelings of pleasure
and pain, while others may be based on a supposed moral feeling
or moral sense. When they are rational, their principle is always
the pursuit of *perfection*, either a perfection to be attained by our
own will or one supposed to be already existent in the will of God
which imposes certain tasks upon our will.

Pages 90–91.—*Empirical principles of heteronomy.*

Since all empirical principles are based on sense and so lack
universality, they are quite unfitted to serve as a basis for moral
law. The principle of seeking one's own happiness is, however,
the most objectionable. We have a right (and even an indirect
duty) to seek our own happiness so far as this is compatible with
moral law; but to be happy is one thing and to be good is another;
and to confuse the two is to abolish the specific distinction between
virtue and vice.

　The doctrine of moral sense has at least the merit of finding
a direct satisfaction in virtue and not merely satisfaction in its
alleged pleasant results. Kant always recognizes the reality of moral
feeling, but he insists that it is a consequence of our recognition of
the law: it cannot itself provide any uniform standard for ourselves
and still less can it legislate for others. The doctrine of moral sense
must in the last resort be classed with doctrines which regard
pleasure or happiness as the only good, since it too finds the good
in the satisfaction of a particular kind of feeling.

Pages 91–93.—*Rational principles of heteronomy.*

The rational principle of perfection as an end to be attained by
us is the best of the proposed heteronomous principles of morality
since it at least appeals to reason for a decision. So far, however,

as it merely bids us aim at the maximum reality appropriate to us, it is utterly vague; and if it includes moral perfection, it is obviously circular. Kant himself holds that the moral law bids us cultivate our natural perfection (the exercise of our talents) and our moral perfection (the doing of duty for duty's sake). His objections are directed against the view that we should obey the moral law for the sake of realizing our own perfection.

The theological principle that to be moral is to obey the perfect will of God must be utterly rejected. If we suppose that God is good, this can only be because we already know what moral goodness is, and our theory is a vicious circle. If, on the other hand, we exclude goodness from our concept of God's will and conceive Him merely as all-powerful, we base morality on fear of an arbitrary, but irresistible, will. A moral system of this kind is in direct opposition to morality. Although morality on Kant's view must lead to religion, it cannot be derived from religion.

Pages 93-95.—*The failure of heteronomy.*

All these doctrines suppose that moral law has to be derived, not from the will itself, but from some object of the will. In being thus heteronomous they can give us no moral or categorical imperative and must consider morally good action to be good, not in itself, but merely as a means to an anticipated result. They thus destroy all *immediate* interest in moral action, and they place man under a law of nature rather than under a law of freedom.

Pages 95-96.—*The position of the argument.*

All Kant claims to have done is to have shown by an analytic argument that the principle of autonomy is the necessary condition of all our moral judgements. If there is such a thing as morality, and if our moral judgements are not merely chimerical, then the principle of autonomy must be accepted. Many thinkers might take this as sufficient proof of the principle, but Kant does not regard such an argument as a proof. He has not even asserted the truth of the principle, still less pretended to prove it.

The principle of autonomy and the corresponding categorical imperative are synthetic *a priori* propositions: they assert that a rational agent—if he had full control over passion—would necessarily act only on maxims by which he can regard himself as making universal law, and that he ought so to act if he is irrational enough to be tempted to act otherwise. Such a proposition requires a synthetic use of pure practical reason, and on this we cannot venture without a critique of this power of reason itself.

OUTLINE OF A CRITIQUE OF PRACTICAL REASON

Pages 97–99.—*Freedom and autonomy.*

When we consider *will* (or practical reason), we may define it as a kind of causality (a power of causal action) belonging to living beings so far as they are rational. To describe such a will as *free* would be to say that it can act causally *without* being caused to do so by something other than itself. Non-rational beings can act causally only so far as they are caused to do so by something other than themselves, and this is what is meant by natural *necessity* as opposed to freedom: if one billiard ball causes another to move, it does so only because it has itself been caused to move by something else.

So far our description of freedom is negative. But a lawless free will would be self-contradictory, and we must make our description positive by saying that a free will would act under laws, but that these laws could not be imposed on it by something other than itself; for, if they were, they would merely be laws of natural necessity. If the laws of freedom cannot be other-imposed (if we may use such an expression), they must be self-imposed. That is to say, freedom would be identical with autonomy; and since autonomy is the principle of morality, a free will would be a will under moral laws.

If then we could presuppose freedom, autonomy, and therefore morality, would follow by mere analysis of the concept of freedom. Nevertheless, as we have seen, the principle of autonomy is a synthetic *a priori* proposition and so can be justified only by bringing in a third term to connect the subject and the predicate of the proposition. The positive concept of freedom furnishes, or directs us to, this third term; but we require further preparation if we are to show what this third term is and to deduce freedom from the concept of pure practical reason.

Pages 99–100.—*Freedom as a necessary presupposition.*

If morality is to be derived from freedom, and if—as we have maintained—morality must be valid for all rational beings as such, it looks as if we have got to prove that the will of a rational being as such is necessarily free. This can never be proved by any experience of merely human action, nor indeed can it be proved at all from the point of view of philosophical theory. For purposes of action, however, it would be enough if we could show that a rational being can act only under the *presupposition* of freedom; for if this were so, the moral laws bound up with freedom would be valid for him just as much as if he were *known* to be free.

Reason as such must necessarily function under the presupposition that it is free both negatively and positively: it must presuppose that it is not determined by outside influences and that it is the source of its own principles. If a rational subject supposed his judgements to be determined, not by rational principles, but by external impulsions, he could not regard these judgements as his own. This must be equally true of practical reason: a rational agent must regard himself as capable of acting on his own rational principles and only so can he regard his will as his own. That is to say, from a practical point of view every rational agent must presuppose his will to be free. Freedom is a necessary presupposition of all action as well as of all thinking.

Pages 101–105.—*Moral interest and the vicious circle.*

We have argued that in action rational beings must presuppose their own freedom and that from this presupposition there necessarily follows the principle of autonomy and consequently the corresponding categorical imperative. In this way we have at least formulated the principle of morality more precisely than has been done before. But why should I simply as a rational being subject myself, and so also other rational beings, to this principle? Why should I attach such supreme value to moral action and feel in this a personal worth in comparison with which pleasure is to count as nothing? Why should I take an interest in moral excellence for its own sake? Have we really given a convincing answer to these difficult questions?

It is no doubt true that we do in fact take an interest in moral excellence, but this interest arises only because we assume that the moral law is binding. We do not as yet see how the moral law can be binding. It may seem that we have fallen into a vicious circle: we have argued that we must suppose ourselves to be free because we are under moral laws and have then argued that we must be under moral laws because we have supposed ourselves to be free. To do this is very far from giving us any justification of the moral law.

Pages 105–110.—*The two standpoints.*

In order to escape from such a vicious circle we must ask ourselves whether we have not two different standpoints (or points of view) from which we may regard our actions. Do we have one standpoint when we conceive ourselves as acting freely and another when we contemplate our actions as observed events?

This doctrine of the two standpoints is an essential part of Kant's Critical Philosophy, which has hitherto been kept in the background. In dealing with it he has to face a difficulty: he cannot assume the elaborate arguments of the *Critique of Pure Reason* to be familiar to his readers nor can he attempt to repeat these elaborate arguments in a short treatise on ethics. He consequently falls back on some rather elementary considerations which, taken by themselves, cannot be very convincing.

All the ideas that are given to our senses come to us without any volition of our own. We assume that these ideas come to us from objects, but by means of ideas so given we can know objects only as they affect ourselves: what these objects are in themselves we do not know. This gives rise to a distinction between things as they appear to us and things as they are in themselves—or again between *appearances* and *things in themselves*. Only appearances can be known by us; but behind appearances we must assume things in themselves, although these things can never be known as they are in themselves, but only as they affect us. This gives us a rough distinction—it is only rough—between a *sensible* world (a world given to sense or at least through sense) and an *intelligible* world (one which we can conceive but never know, since all human knowledge requires a combination of sensing and conceiving).

This distinction applies also to man's knowledge of himself.

By inner sense (or introspection) he can know himself only as he appears, but behind this appearance he must assume that there is an Ego as it is in itself. So far as he is known by inner sense, and indeed so far as he is capable of receiving sensations passively, man must regard himself as belonging to the sensible world. So far, however, as he may be capable of pure activity apart from sense, he must regard himself as belonging to the intelligible world. The intelligible world is here described as an 'intellectual' world—a world which is intelligible because it is intelligent—although it is added that of this world we can know nothing further.

Now man actually finds in himself a pure activity apart from sense. He finds in himself a power of reason. Here, it should be noted, Kant appeals first, as he did before, to theoretical reason, although he now takes reason in his own special Critical sense. We have a spontaneous power of 'understanding' which (no doubt along with other factors) produces from itself such concepts (or *categories*) as that of cause and effect and uses these concepts to bring the ideas of sense under rules. Thus in spite of its genuine spontaneity understanding is still bound up with sense, and apart from sense it would think nothing at all. 'Reason', on the other hand, is a power of *Ideas*—that is, it produces concepts (of the unconditioned) which go beyond sense altogether and can have no examples given to sense. Unlike understanding, reason shows a pure spontaneity which is entirely independent of sense.

In virtue of this spontaneity man must conceive himself as belonging, *qua* intelligence, to the intelligible world and as subject to laws which have their ground in reason alone. So far as he is sensuous and is known to himself by means of inner sense he must regard himself as belonging to the sensible world and as subject to the laws of nature. These are the two standpoints from which a finite rational being must view himself.

This doctrine applies equally to pure practical reason. Since from one standpoint man, as a finite rational being, must conceive himself as belonging to the intelligible world, he must conceive his will as free from determination by sensuous causes and as obedient to laws having their ground in reason alone. To say this is to say that he can never conceive the causal action of his own will except under the Idea of freedom. Thus he must, as a rational being, act only on the presupposition of freedom, and from this there follows, as we have seen, the principle of autonomy and the categorical imperative.

The suspicion of a vicious circle is now removed. From the standpoint of a rational agent who conceives himself as free and as a member of the intelligible world, man must recognize the principle of autonomy. When he thinks of himself as a member of both the intelligible and the sensible world, he must recognize the principle of autonomy as a categorical imperative.

In all this Kant does not make it wholly clear whether his inference is from membership of the intelligible world to freedom or *vice versa*. It might well be suggested that we conceive ourselves as free in action and so as members of the intelligible world only because we already recognize the principle of autonomy and the categorical imperative; and indeed this appears to be Kant's own view in the *Critique of Practical Reason*. Nevertheless, his comparison between pure theoretical reason and pure practical reason is of very great interest; and we must remember that just as pure theoretical reason conceives Ideas of the unconditioned, so pure practical reason seeks in action to realize the Idea of an unconditioned law.

Pages 110-112.—*How is a categorical imperative possible?*

As a finite rational agent man must regard himself from two standpoints—first as a member of the intelligible world, and secondly as a member of the sensible world. If I were solely a member of the intelligible world, all my actions would necessarily accord with the principle of autonomy; if I were solely a part of the sensible world, they would necessarily be entirely subject to the law of nature. At this point unfortunately we come to an argument which may be new but is certainly confused in expression and hard to interpret. *The intelligible world contains the ground of the sensible world and also of its laws.* From this premise (which itself demands considerable expansion) Kant appears to infer that the law governing my will as a member of the intelligible world *ought* to govern my will in spite of the fact that I am also (from another point of view) a member of the sensible world.

This looks like a metaphysical argument from the superior reality of the intelligible world and so of the rational will, but such an interpretation seems to be immediately repudiated by

Kant. The categorical 'I ought', we are told, is a synthetic *a priori* proposition; and the third term which connects this 'ought' with the will of an imperfectly rational agent like myself is the *Idea* of the same will, viewed, however, as a pure will belonging to the intelligible world. This *Idea* is apparently the third term to which freedom was said to direct us at the end of the first section of the present chapter: it may indeed be described as a more precise Idea of freedom—that is, of a free will. Its function is said to be roughly similar to that played by the categories in the synthetic *a priori* propositions which are necessary for our experience of nature.

This doctrine is confirmed by an appeal to our ordinary moral consciousness as present even in a bad man. The moral 'I ought' is really an 'I will' for man regarded as a member of the intelligible world. It is conceived as an 'I ought' only because he considers himself to be also a member of the sensible world—and so subject to the hindrances of sensuous desires.

Pages 113–115.—*The antinomy of freedom and necessity.*

Kant's argument obviously raises the problem of freedom and necessity. This problem constitutes what Kant calls an 'antinomy'— that is to say, we are faced with mutually conflicting propositions each of which appears to be the necessary conclusion of an irrefutable argument.

The concept of freedom is an Idea of reason without which there could be no moral judgements, just as the concept of natural necessity (or of cause and effect) is a category of the understanding without which there could be no knowledge of nature. Yet the two concepts are apparently incompatible with each other. According to the first concept our actions must be free; and according to the second concept our actions (as events in the known world of nature) must be governed by the laws of cause and effect. Reason has to show that there is no genuine contradiction between the two concepts or else to abandon freedom in favour of natural necessity, which has at least the advantage of being confirmed in experience.

Pages 115–118.—*The two standpoints.*

It would be impossible to resolve the contradiction if we conceived of ourselves as free and as determined in the same sense and in the same relationship. We have to show that the contradiction arises from conceiving ourselves in two different senses and relationships and that from this double standpoint these two characteristics not only can, but must, be combined in the same subject. This task is incumbent on speculative philosophy if practical (or moral) philosophy is to be freed from damaging external attacks.

The two standpoints in question are those we have already encountered. Man must—from different points of view—consider himself both as a member of the intelligible world and as a part of the sensible world. Once this is grasped the contradiction disappears. Man can, and indeed must, consider himself to be free as a member of the intelligible world and determined as a part of the sensible world; nor is there any contradiction in supposing that as an *appearance* in the sensible world he is subject to laws which do not apply to him as a *thing in itself.* Thus man does not consider himself responsible for his desires and inclinations, but he does consider himself responsible for indulging them to the detriment of the moral law.

In this passage Kant speaks as if we *know* the intelligible world to be governed by reason. This unguarded statement he immediately proceeds to qualify.

Pages 118–120.—*There is no knowledge of the intelligible world.*

In thus *conceiving* the intelligible world and so *thinking itself into* the intelligible world practical reason does not overstep its limits: it would do this only if it claimed to *know* the intelligible world and so to *intuit itself into* the intelligible world (since all human knowledge requires sensuous intuition as well as concepts). Our thought of the intelligible world is negative—that is to say, it is only the thought of a world which is *not* known through sense. It enables us, however, not only to conceive the will as negatively free (free from determination by sensuous causes), but also to conceive it as positively free (free to act on its own principle of autonomy). Without this concept of the intelligible world we should have to regard our will as completely determined by sensuous causes, and consequently this concept (or point of view) is necessary if we are to regard our will as rational and so far as free. Admittedly when we think ourselves into the intelligible world our thought carries with it the Idea of an order and a law different from that of the world of sense: it becomes necessary for us to conceive the intelligible world as the totality of rational beings considered as things in themselves. Nevertheless this is not a claim to knowledge of the intelligible world: it is merely a claim to conceive it as compatible with the formal condition of morality—the principle of autonomy.

Pages 120–121.—*There is no explanation of freedom.*

Reason would overstep all its limits if it pretended to explain how freedom is possible or, in other words, to explain how pure reason can be practical.

The only things we can explain are objects of experience, and to explain them is to bring them under the laws of nature (the laws of cause and effect). Freedom, however, is merely an Idea: it does not supply us with examples which can be known by experience and can be brought under the law of cause and effect. We obviously cannot explain a free action by pointing out its cause, and this means that we cannot explain it at all. All we can do is to *defend* freedom against the attacks of those who claim to know that freedom is impossible. Those who do this very properly apply the laws of nature to man considered as an appearance; but they continue to regard him as an appearance when they are asked to conceive him, *qua* intelligence, as also a thing in himself. To insist on considering man only from one point of view is admittedly to exclude the possibility of regarding him as both free and determined; but the seeming contradiction would fall away if they were willing to reflect that things in themselves must lie behind appearances as their ground and that the laws governing things in themselves need not be the same as the laws governing their appearances.

Pages 121–123.—*There is no explanation of moral interest.*

To say that we cannot explain how freedom is possible is also to say that we cannot explain how it is possible to take an interest in the moral law.

An interest arises only through a combination of feeling and reason. A sensuous impulse becomes an interest only when it is conceived by reason, and consequently interests are found only in finite rational agents who are also sensuous. Interests may be regarded as the motives of human action, but we must remember that there are two kinds of interest. When the interest is based on the feeling and desire aroused by some object of experience, we may be said to have a mediate (or pathological) interest in the action appropriate to attain the object. When the interest is aroused by the Idea of the moral law, we may be said to take an immediate (or practical) interest in the action willed in accordance with this Idea.

The basis of the interest we take in moral action is what is called 'moral feeling'. This feeling is the result of recognizing the binding character of the moral law and not—as is often held—the gauge of our moral judgements.

This means that pure reason by its Idea of the moral law must be the cause of a moral feeling which can be regarded as the sensuous motive of moral action. We have here a special kind of causality—the causality of a mere Idea—and it is alway impossible to know a priori what cause will produce what effect. In order to determine the cause of any effect we must have recourse to experience; but experience can discover the relation of cause and effect only between two objects of experience; and in this case the cause is not an object of experience, but is, on the contrary, a mere Idea which can have no object in experience. Hence it is impossible to explain moral interest—that is, to explain why we should take an interest in the universality of our maxim as a law. This doctrine, it may be added, does not appear to be self-consistent, and a different view is taken in the *Critique of Practical Reason*.

The really important point is that the moral law is not valid merely because it interests us. On the contrary, it interests us because we recognize it to be valid.

Kant concludes by saying that the moral law is valid because it springs from our own will as intelligence and so from our proper self; '*but what belongs to mere appearance is necessarily subordinated by reason to the character of the thing in itself*'.

This looks like a metaphysical argument for morality, one based on the superior reality of the intelligible world and so of the rational will. This type of argument seemed to be suggested also (although immediately repudiated) in the section '*How is a categorical imperative possible?*' In the main, however, Kant's metaphysics rests on his ethics rather than *vice versa*.

Pages 124–126.—*General review of the argument.*

We must now turn back to our main question 'How is a categorical imperative possible?' We have answered this question so far as we have shown that it is possible only on the presupposition of freedom and that this presupposition is one which is necessary for rational agents as such. From this presupposition there follows the principle of autonomy and so of the categorical imperative; and this is sufficient for purposes of action—sufficient to convince us of the validity of the categorical imperative as a principle of action. We have also shown that it is not only possible to pre-suppose freedom without contradicting the necessity which must prevail in the world of nature, but that it is also objectively necessary for a rational agent conscious of possessing reason and a will to make this presupposition the condition of all his actions. We cannot, however, explain how freedom is possible, how pure reason by itself can be practical, or how we can take a moral interest in the mere validity of our maxims as universal laws.

We can explain things only by showing them to be the effects of some cause, and this kind of explanation is here excluded. Kant is careful to insist that it is impossible to use the intelligible world as the basis for the required explanation. He is so often charged with doing precisely this that his statement here is worthy of very close attention. I have a necessary Idea of the intelligible world, but it is only an Idea: I can have no knowledge of this world since I have, and can have, no *acquaintance* with such a world (by means of intuition). My Idea of it signifies only a world *not* accessible to our senses—a 'something more' beyond the world of sense: if we could not conceive this 'something more', we should have to say that all action is determined by sensuous motives. Even of the *pure reason* which conceives the Idea or Ideal of the intelligible world (and which also conceives itself as a member of such a world) we have still only an *Idea*: we have only a concept of its form (the principle of autonomy) and a corresponding concept of it as causing actions solely in virtue of its form. Here all sensuous motives are removed, and a mere Idea would itself have to be the motive of moral action. To make this intelligible *a priori* is altogether beyond our powers.

Pages 126–127.—*The extreme limit of moral enquiry.*

With this Idea of an intelligible world as a something more and other than the sensible world we come to the extreme limit of all moral enquiry. To fix this limit is, however, of the utmost practical importance. Unless we see that the world of sense is not the whole of reality, reason will never be kept from trying to discover empirical interests as a basis for morality—a proceeding fatal to morality itself. And unless we see that we can have no knowledge of the 'something more' beyond the world of sense, reason will never be kept from fluttering about impotently in a space which for it is empty—the space of transcendent concepts known to it as 'the intelligible world'—and so from getting lost among mere phantoms of the brain. Empirical and mystical theories of morality can alike be got rid of only when we have determined the limit of moral enquiry.

Yet although all *knowledge* ends when we come to the limit of the sensible world, the Idea of the intelligible world as a whole of all intelligences may serve the purpose of a rational *belief*; and it may arouse a lively interest in the moral law by means of the splendid ideal of a universal kingdom of ends.

Pages 127–128.—*Concluding note.*

In his final note Kant gives some indication of the character of 'reason' in his own technical sense. Reason cannot be satisfied with the merely contingent and always seeks for knowledge of the necessary. But it can grasp the necessary only by finding its condition. Unless the condition is itself necessary reason must still be unsatisfied, so it must seek the condition of the condition and so on *ad infinitum*. Thus it is bound to conceive the Idea of the *totality* of conditions—a totality which, if it is a totality, can have no further conditions and so must be *unconditionally necessary* if there is to be anything necessary at all. Such an Idea of the unconditionally necessary cannot, however, give us knowledge since it has no corresponding sensible object.

We have seen that pure practical reason must similarly conceive a law of action which is unconditionally necessary and is therefore a categorical imperative (for imperfectly rational agents). If we can comprehend a necessity only by discovering its condition, an unconditioned necessity must be incomprehensible. Hence Kant concludes—with an unnecessary appearance of paradox—that the unconditioned necessity of the categorical imperative must be incomprehensible, but that we can comprehend its incomprehensibility.

The practical point of all this is that it is absurd to ask why we should do our duty (or obey the categorical imperative) and to expect as an answer that we should do so because of *something else*—some interest or satisfaction of our own in this world or the next. If such an answer could be given, it would mean that no imperatives were categorical and that duty is a mere illusion.

GROUNDWORK

OF THE

METAPHYSIC OF MORALS

BY

IMMANUEL KANT

[*The different branches of philosophy.*]

ANCIENT Greek philosophy was divided into three sciences: *physics*, *ethics*, and *logic*. This division fits the nature of the subject perfectly, and there is no need to improve on it—except perhaps by adding the principle on which it is based. By so doing we may be able on the one hand to guarantee its completeness and on the other to determine correctly its necessary subdivisions.

All rational knowledge is either *material* and concerned with some object, or *formal* and concerned solely with the form of understanding and reason themselves—with the universal rules of thinking as such without regard to differences in its objects. Formal philosophy is called *logic;* while material philosophy, which has ii to do with determinate objects and with the laws to which they are subject, is in turn divided into two, since the laws in question are laws either of *nature* or of *freedom*. The science of the first is called *physics*, that of the second *ethics*. The former is also called natural philosophy, the latter moral philosophy.

Logic can have no empirical part[1]—that is, no part in which the universal and necessary laws of thinking are based on grounds taken from experience. Otherwise it would not be logic—that is, it would not be a canon for understanding and reason, valid for all thinking and capable of demonstration. As against this, both natural and moral philosophy can each have an empirical part, since the former has to formulate its laws for nature as an object of experience, and the latter for the will of man so far as affected by nature—the first set of laws being those in accordance with which everything happens, the second being those in accordance 388] iii with which everything ought to happen, although they also take into account the conditions under which what ought to happen very often does not happen.

All philosophy so far as it rests on the basis of experience can be called *empirical* philosophy. If it sets forth its doctrines as depending entirely on *a priori* principles, it can be called *pure* philosophy. The latter when wholly formal is called *logic*; but if it is confined to determinate objects of the understanding, it is then called *metaphysics*.

In this way there arises the Idea of a two-fold metaphysic—
a metaphysic of nature and *a metaphysic of morals*. Thus physics will
have its empirical part, but it will also have a rational one; and
likewise ethics—although here the empirical part might be called
specifically *practical anthropology*, while the rational part might
properly be called *morals*.

[*The need for pure ethics.*]

All industries, arts, and crafts have gained by the division of
iv labour—that is to say, one man no longer does everything, but
each confines himself to a particular task, differing markedly from
others in its technique, so that he may be able to perform it with
the highest perfection and with greater ease. Where tasks are not
so distinguished and divided, where every man is a jack of all
trades, there industry is still sunk in utter barbarism. In itself it
might well be a subject not unworthy of examination, if we asked
whether pure philosophy in all its parts does not demand its own
special craftsman. Would it not be better for the whole of this
learned industry if those accustomed to purvey, in accordance
with the public taste, a mixture of the empirical and the rational
in various proportions unknown even to themselves—the self-styled
'creative thinkers' as opposed to the 'hair-splitters' who attend to
the purely rational part—were to be warned against carrying on
at once two jobs very different in their technique, each perhaps
v requiring a special talent and the combination of both in one
person producing mere bunglers? Here, however, I confine myself
to asking whether the nature of science does not always require
that the empirical part should be scrupulously separated from the
rational one, and that (empirical) physics proper should be prefaced
by a metaphysic of nature, while practical anthropology should be
prefaced by a metaphysic of morals—each metaphysic having to
be scrupulously cleansed of everything empirical if we are to know
389 how much pure reason can accomplish in both cases and from
what sources it can by itself draw its own *a priori* teaching. I leave
it an open question whether the latter business[1] is to be conducted
by all moralists (whose name is legion) or only by those who feel
a vocation for the subject.

Since my aim here is directed strictly to moral philosophy, I limit my proposed question to this point only—Do we not think it a matter of the utmost necessity to work out for once a pure moral philosophy completely cleansed of everything that can only vi be empirical and appropriate to anthropology?[1] That there must be such a philosophy is already obvious from the common Idea[2] of duty and from the laws of morality. Every one must admit that a law has to carry with it absolute necessity if it is to be valid morally—valid, that is, as a ground of obligation; that the command 'Thou shalt not lie' could not hold merely for men, other rational beings having no obligation to abide by it—and similarly with all other genuine moral laws; that here consequently the ground of obligation must be looked for, not in the nature of man nor in the circumstances of the world in which he is placed, but solely *a priori* in the concepts of pure reason; and that every other precept based on principles of mere experience—and even a precept that may in a certain sense be considered universal, so far as it rests in its slightest part, perhaps only in its motive, on empirical grounds[3] —can indeed be called a practical rule, but never a moral law.

Thus in practical knowledge as a whole, not only are moral vii laws, together with their principles, essentially different from all the rest in which there is some empirical element, but the whole of moral philosophy is based entirely on the part of it that is pure. When applied to man it does not borrow in the slightest from acquaintance with him (in anthropology), but gives him laws *a priori* as a rational being.[1] These laws admittedly require in addition a power of judgement sharpened by experience, partly in order to distinguish the cases to which they apply, partly to procure for them admittance to the will of man and influence over practice; for man, affected as he is by so many inclinations,[2] is capable of the Idea of a pure practical reason, but he has not so easily the power to realize the Idea *in concreto* in his conduct of life.

A metaphysic of morals is thus indispensably necessary, not merely in order to investigate, from motives of speculation, the source of practical principles which are present *a priori* in our 390] viii reason, but because morals themselves remain exposed to corruption of all sorts as long as this guiding thread is lacking, this ultimate norm for correct moral judgement. For if any action is to be morally good, it is not enough that it should *conform* to the moral law—

it must also be done *for the sake of the moral law*: where this is not so, the conformity is only too contingent and precarious, since the non-moral ground at work will now and then produce actions which accord with the law, but very often actions which transgress it. Now the moral law in its purity and genuineness (and in the field of action it is precisely this that matters most) is to be looked for nowhere else than in a pure philosophy. Hence pure philosophy (that is, metaphysics[1]) must come first, and without it there can be no moral philosophy at all. Indeed a philosophy which mixes up these pure principles with empirical ones does not deserve the name of philosophy (since philosophy is distinguished from ordinary rational knowledge precisely because it sets forth in a separate science what the latter apprehends only as confused with other ix things). Still less does it deserve the name of moral philosophy, since by this very confusion it undermines even the purity of morals themselves and acts against its own proper purpose.

[*The philosophy of willing as such.*]

It must not be imagined that in the propaedeutics prefixed to his moral philosophy by the celebrated *Wolff*—that is, in the '*Universal Practical Philosophy*',[1] as he called it—we already have what is here demanded and consequently do not need to break entirely new ground. Precisely because it was supposed to be a universal practical philosophy, it has taken into consideration, not a special kind of will—not such a will as is completely determined by *a priori* principles apart from any empirical motives and so can be called a pure will—but willing as such, together with all activities and conditions belonging to it in this general sense. Because of this it differs from a metaphysic of morals in the same way as general x logic differs from transcendental philosophy, the first of which sets forth the activities and rules of thinking *as such*, while the second expounds the special activities and rules of *pure* thinking— that is, of the thinking whereby objects are known completely *a priori*;[1] for a metaphysic of morals has to investigate the Idea and principles of a possible *pure* will, and not the activities and conditions of human willing as such, which are drawn for the most part from 391 psychology. The fact that in this 'universal practical philosophy' there is also talk (though quite unjustifiably) about moral laws and duty is no objection to what I say. For the authors of this science remain true to their Idea of it on this point as well: they do not distinguish motives which, as such, are conceived completely *a priori* by reason alone and are genuinely moral, from empirical motives which understanding raises to general concepts by the mere comparison of experiences. On the contrary, without taking into account differences in their origin they consider motives only **xi** as regards their relative strength or weakness (looking upon all of them as homogeneous) and construct on this basis their concept of *obligation*. This concept is anything but moral; but its character is only such as is to be expected from a philosophy which never decides, as regards the *source* of all practical concepts, whether they arise only *a posteriori* or arise *a priori* as well.

[*The aim of the* Groundwork.]

Intending, as I do, to publish some day a metaphysic of morals, I issue this *Groundwork* in advance. For such a metaphysic there is strictly no other foundation than a critique of *pure practical reason*, just as for metaphysics[1] there is no other foundation than the critique of pure speculative reason which I have already published. Yet, on the one hand, there is not the same extreme necessity for the former critique as for the latter, since human reason can, in matters of morality, be easily brought to a high degree of accuracy and precision even in the most ordinary intelligence, whereas in its theoretical, but pure, activity it is, on the contrary, out and out dialectical;[1] and, on the other hand, a critique **xii** of practical reason, if it is to be complete, requires, on my view, that we should be able at the same time to show the unity of practical and theoretical reason in a common principle, since in the end there can only be one and the same reason, which must be differentiated solely in its application. Here, however, I found myself as yet unable to bring my work to such completeness without introducing considerations of quite another sort and so confusing the reader. This is why, instead of calling it a '*Critique of Pure Practical Reason*', I have adopted the title '*Groundwork of the Metaphysic of Morals*'.

But, in the third place, since a metaphysic of morals, in spite of its horrifying title, can be in a high degree popular and suited to the ordinary intelligence, I think it useful to issue separately this preparatory work on its foundations so that later I need not insert the subtleties inevitable in these matters into doctrines more 392] **xiii** easy to understand.

The sole aim of the present Groundwork is to seek out and establish *the supreme principle of morality*. This by itself is a business which by its very purpose constitutes a whole and has to be separated off from every other enquiry. The application of the principle to the whole system would no doubt throw much light on my answers to this central question, so important and yet hitherto so far from being satisfactorily discussed; and the adequacy it manifests throughout would afford it strong confirmation. All the same, I had to forego this advantage, which in any case would be more flattering to myself than helpful to others, since the convenience of a principle in use and its seeming adequacy afford no completely safe proof of its correctness. They rather awaken a certain bias against examining and weighing it in all strictness for itself without any regard to its consequences.

[*The method of the* Groundwork.]

xiv   The method I have adopted in this book is, I believe, one which will work best if we proceed analytically from common knowledge to the formulation of its supreme principle and then back again synthetically from an examination of this principle and its origins to the common knowledge in which we find its application. Hence the division turns out to be as follows:—

1. *Chapter I:* Passage from ordinary rational knowledge of morality to philosophical.
2. *Chapter II:* Passage from popular moral philosophy to a metaphysic of morals.
3. *Chapter III:* Final step from a metaphysic of morals to a critique of pure practical reason.

PASSAGE FROM ORDINARY RATIONAL KNOWLEDGE OF MORALITY TO PHILOSOPHICAL

[The good will.]

IT is impossible to conceive anything at all in the world, or even out of it, which can be taken as good without qualification, except a *good will*. Intelligence, wit, judgement, and any other *talents* of the mind we may care to name, or courage, resolution, and constancy of purpose, as qualities of *temperament*, are without doubt good and desirable in many respects; but they can also be extremely bad and hurtful when the will is not good which has to make use of these gifts of nature, and which for this reason has the term '*character*' applied to its peculiar quality. It is exactly the same with *gifts of fortune*. Power, wealth, honour, even health and that complete well-being and contentment with one's state which goes by the name of '*happiness*', produce boldness, and as a consequence 2 often over-boldness as well, unless a good will is present by which their influence on the mind—and so too the whole principle of action—may be corrected and adjusted to universal ends; not to mention that a rational and impartial spectator can never feel approval in contemplating the uninterrupted prosperity of a being graced by no touch of a pure and good will, and that consequently a good will seems to constitute the indispensable condition of our very worthiness to be happy.

Some qualities are even helpful to this good will itself and can make its task very much easier.[1] They have none the less no inner unconditioned worth, but rather presuppose a good will which 394 sets a limit to the esteem in which they are rightly held[2] and does not permit us to regard them as absolutely good. Moderation in affections and passions,[3] self-control, and sober reflexion are not only good in many respects: they may even seem to constitute part of the *inner* worth of a person. Yet they are far from being properly described as good without qualification (however unconditionally they have been commended by the ancients). For with-

out the principles of a good will they may become exceedingly
3 bad; and the very coolness of a scoundrel makes him, not merely
more dangerous, but also immediately more abominable in our
eyes than we should have taken him to be without it.

[*The good will and its results.*]

A good will is not good because of what it effects or accomplishes—because of its fitness for attaining some proposed end:
it is good through its willing alone—that is, good in itself. Considered in itself it is to be esteemed beyond comparison as far
higher than anything it could ever bring about merely in order to
favour some inclination or, if you like, the sum total of inclinations.
Even if, by some special disfavour of destiny or by the niggardly
endowment of step-motherly nature, this will is entirely lacking
in power to carry out its intentions; if by its utmost effort it still
accomplishes nothing, and only good will is left (not, admittedly,
as a mere wish, but as the straining of every means so far as they
are in our control); even then it would still shine like a jewel for
its own sake as something which has its full value in itself. Its usefulness or fruitlessness can neither add to, nor subtract from, this
value. Its usefulness would be merely, as it were, the setting which
enables us to handle it better in our ordinary dealings or to attract
4 the attention of those not yet sufficiently expert, but not to
commend it to experts or to determine its value.

[*The function of reason.*]

Yet in this Idea of the absolute value of a mere will, all useful
results being left out of account in its assessment, there is something
so strange that, in spite of all the agreement it receives even from
ordinary reason, there must arise the suspicion that perhaps its
secret basis is merely some high-flown fantasticality, and that we
may have misunderstood the purpose of nature in attaching reason
395 to our will as its governor. We will therefore submit our Idea to
an examination from this point of view.

In the natural constitution of an organic being—that is, of one
contrived for the purpose of life—let us take it as a principle that
in it no organ is to be found for any end unless it is also the most
appropriate to that end and the best fitted for it. Suppose now

that for a being possessed of reason and a will the real purpose of nature were his *preservation*, his *welfare*, or in a word his *happiness*. In that case nature would have hit on a very bad arrangement by choosing reason in the creature to carry out this purpose. For all the actions he has to perform with this end in view, and the whole 5 rule of his behaviour, would have been mapped out for him far more accurately by instinct; and the end in question could have been maintained far more surely by instinct than it ever can be by reason. If reason should have been imparted to this favoured creature as well, it would have had to serve him only for contemplating the happy disposition of his nature, for admiring it, for enjoying it, and for being grateful to its beneficent Cause—not for subjecting his power of appetition to such feeble and defective guidance or for meddling incompetently with the purposes of nature. In a word, nature would have prevented reason from striking out into a *practical use* and from presuming, with its feeble vision, to think out for itself a plan for happiness and for the means to its attainment. Nature would herself have taken over the choice, not only of ends, but also of means, and would with wise precaution have entrusted both to instinct alone.

In actual fact too we find that the more a cultivated reason concerns itself with the aim of enjoying life and happiness, the farther does man get away from true contentment. This is why there arises in many, and that too in those who have made most trial of this use of reason, if they are only candid enough to admit 6 it, a certain degree of *misology*—that is, a hatred of reason;[1] for when they balance all the advantage they draw, I will not say from thinking out all the arts of ordinary indulgence, but even from science (which in the last resort seems to them to be also an indulgence of the mind), they discover that they have in fact only brought more trouble on their heads than they have gained in the 396 way of happiness. On this account they come to envy, rather than to despise, the more common run of men, who are closer to the guidance of mere natural instinct, and who do not allow their reason to have much influence on their conduct. So far we must admit that the judgement of those who seek to moderate—and even to reduce below zero—the conceited glorification of such advantages as reason is supposed to provide in the way of happiness and contentment with life is in no way soured or ungrateful to the goodness with which the world is governed. These judgements rather have as their hidden ground the Idea of another and much more worthy purpose of existence, for which, and not for happiness, reason is quite properly designed, and to which, therefore, as a supreme condition the private purposes of man must for the most part be subordinated.

For since reason is not sufficiently serviceable for guiding the 7 will safely as regards its objects and the satisfaction of all our needs (which it in part even multiplies)—a purpose for which an implanted natural instinct would have led us much more surely; and since none the less reason has been imparted to us as a practical power—that is, as one which is to have influence on the *will*; its true function must be to produce a *will* which is *good*, not as a *means* to some further end, but *in itself*; and for this function reason was absolutely necessary in a world where nature, in distributing her aptitudes, has everywhere else gone to work in a purposive manner. Such a will need not on this account be the sole and complete good,[1] but it must be the highest good and the condition of all the rest, even of all our demands for happiness. In that case we can easily reconcile with the wisdom of nature our observation that the cultivation of reason which is required for the first and unconditioned purpose may in many ways, at least in this life, restrict the attainment of the second purpose—namely, happiness—which is always conditioned; and indeed that it can even reduce happiness to less than zero without nature proceeding contrary to its purpose; for reason, which recognizes as its highest practical function the establishment of a good will, in attaining this end is capable only of its own peculiar kind of contentment[2] —contentment in fulfilling a purpose which in turn is determined 8 by reason alone, even if this fulfilment should often involve interference with the purposes of inclination.

[The good will and duty.]

397   We have now to elucidate the concept of a will estimable in itself and good apart from any further end. This concept, which is already present in a sound natural understanding and requires not so much to be taught as merely to be clarified, always holds the highest place in estimating the total worth of our actions and

constitutes the condition of all the rest. We will therefore take
up the concept of *duty*, which includes that of a good will, exposed,
however, to certain subjective limitations and obstacles. These, so
far from hiding a good will or disguising it, rather bring it out
by contrast and make it shine forth more brightly.[1]

[The motive of duty.]

I will here pass over all actions already recognized as contrary
to duty, however useful they may be with a view to this or that
end; for about these the question does not even arise whether
they could have been done *for the sake of duty* inasmuch as they
are directly opposed to it. I will also set aside actions which in
fact accord with duty, yet for which men have *no immediate
inclination*, but perform them because impelled to do so by some
other inclination. For there it is easy to decide whether the action 9
which accords with duty has been done *from duty* or from some
purpose of self-interest. This distinction is far more difficult to
perceive when the action accords with duty and the subject has
in addition an *immediate* inclination to the action. For example,[1]
it certainly accords with duty that a grocer should not overcharge
his inexperienced customer; and where there is much competition
a sensible shopkeeper refrains from so doing and keeps to a fixed
and general price for everybody so that a child can buy from him
just as well as anyone else. Thus people are served *honestly*; but this
is not nearly enough to justify us in believing that the shopkeeper
has acted in this way from duty or from principles of fair dealing;
his interests required him to do so. We cannot assume him to have
in addition an immediate inclination towards his customers, leading
him, as it were out of love, to give no man preference over another
in the matter of price. Thus the action was done neither from
duty nor from immediate inclination, but solely from purposes
of self-interest.

On the other hand, to preserve one's life is a duty, and besides
this every one has also an immediate inclination to do so. But
on account of this the often anxious precautions taken by the
greater part of mankind for this purpose have no inner worth,
and the maxim[2] of their action is without moral content. They do 398
protect their lives *in conformity with duty*, but not *from the motive* 10
of duty. When on the contrary, disappointments and hopeless

misery have quite taken away the taste for life; when a wretched man, strong in soul and more angered at his fate than faint-hearted or cast down, longs for death and still preserves his life without loving it—not from inclination or fear but from duty; then indeed his maxim has a moral content.

To help others where one can is a duty, and besides this there are many spirits of so sympathetic a temper that, without any further motive of vanity or self-interest, they find an inner pleasure in spreading happiness around them and can take delight in the contentment of others as their own work. Yet I maintain that in such a case an action of this kind, however right and however amiable it may be, has still no genuinely moral worth. It stands on the same footing as other inclinations[1]—for example, the inclination for honour, which if fortunate enough to hit on something beneficial and right and consequently honourable, deserves praise and encouragement, but not esteem; for its maxim lacks moral content, namely, the performance of such actions, not from inclination, but *from duty*. Suppose then that the mind of this friend of man were overclouded by sorrows of his own which extinguished all sympathy with the fate of others, but that he still had power to help those in distress, though no longer stirred by the need of others because sufficiently occupied with his own; and suppose that, when no longer moved by any inclination, he tears himself out of this deadly insensibility and does the action without any inclination for the sake of duty alone; then for the first time his action has its genuine moral worth. Still further: if nature had implanted little sympathy in this or that man's heart; if (being in other respects an honest fellow) he were cold in temperament and indifferent to the sufferings of others—perhaps because, being endowed with the special gift of patience and robust endurance in his own sufferings, he assumed the like in others or even demanded it; if such a man (who would in truth not be the worst product of nature) were not exactly fashioned by her to be a philanthropist, would he not still find in himself a source from which he might draw a worth far higher than any that a good-natured temperament can have? Assuredly he would. It is precisely in this that the worth of character begins to show —a moral worth and beyond all comparison the highest—namely, that he does good, not from inclination, but from duty.

To assure one's own happiness is a duty (at least indirectly); for discontent with one's state, in a press of cares and amidst unsatis- 12 fied wants, might easily become a great *temptation to the transgression of duty*. But here also, apart from regard to duty, all men have already of themselves the strongest and deepest inclination towards happiness, because precisely in this Idea of happiness all inclinations are combined into a sum total.[1] The prescription for happiness is, however, often so constituted as greatly to interfere with some inclinations, and yet men cannot form under the name of 'happiness' any determinate and assured conception of the satisfaction of all inclinations as a sum. Hence it is not to be wondered at that a single inclination which is determinate as to what it promises and as to the time of its satisfaction may outweigh a wavering Idea; and that a man, for example, a sufferer from gout, may choose to enjoy what he fancies and put up with what he can—on the ground that on balance he has here at least not killed the enjoyment of the present moment because of some possibly groundless expectations of the good fortune supposed to attach to soundness of health. But in this case also, when the universal inclination towards happiness has failed to determine his will, when good health, at least for him, has not entered into his calculations as so necessary, what remains over, here as in other cases, is a law—the law of furthering his happiness, not from inclination, 13 but from duty; and in this for the first time his conduct has a real moral worth.

It is doubtless in this sense that we should understand too the passages from Scripture in which we are commanded to love our neighbour and even our enemy. For love out of inclination cannot be commanded; but kindness done from duty—although no inclination impels us, and even although natural and unconquerable disinclination stands in our way—is *practical*, and not *pathological*, love, residing in the will and not in the propensions of feeling, in principles of action and not of melting compassion; and it is this practical love alone which can be an object of command.

[*The formal principle of duty.*]

Our second proposition[1] is this: An action done from duty has its moral worth, *not in the purpose* to be attained by it, but in

the maxim in accordance with which it is decided upon; it depends
400 therefore, not on the realization of the object of the action, but
solely on the *principle* of *volition* in accordance with which,
irrespective of all objects of the faculty of desire,[2] the action has
been performed. That the purposes we may have in our actions,
and also their effects considered as ends and motives of the will,
can give to actions no unconditioned and moral worth is clear
from what has gone before. Where then can this worth be found
14 if we are not to find it in the will's relation to the effect hoped for
from the action? It can be found nowhere but *in the principle of
the will*, irrespective of the ends which can be brought about by
such an action; for between its *a priori* principle, which is formal,
and its *a posteriori* motive, which is material, the will stands, so to
speak, at a parting of the ways; and since it must be determined
by some principle, it will have to be determined by the formal
principle of volition when an action is done from duty, where,
as we have seen, every material principle is taken away from it.

[Reverence for the law.]

Our third proposition, as an inference from the two preceding,
I would express thus: *Duty is the necessity to act out of reverence
for the law.* For an object as the effect of my proposed action I can
have an *inclination*, but *never reverence*, precisely because it is merely
the effect, and not the activity, of a will. Similarly for inclination
as such, whether my own or that of another, I cannot have
reverence: I can at most in the first case approve, and in the second
case sometimes even love—that is, regard it as favourable to my
own advantage. Only something which is conjoined with my
will solely as a ground and never as an effect—something which
does not serve my inclination, but outweighs it or at least leaves
15 it entirely out of account in my choice—and therefore only bare
law for its own sake, can be an object of reverence and therewith
a command. Now an action done from duty has to set aside
altogether the influence of inclination, and along with inclination
every object of the will; so there is nothing left able to determine
the will except objectively the *law* and subjectively *pure reverence*

for this practical law, and therefore the maxim* of obeying this law even to the detriment of all my inclinations. 401

Thus the moral worth of an action does not depend on the result expected from it, and so too does not depend on any principle of action that needs to borrow its motive from this expected result. For all these results (agreeable states and even the promotion of happiness in others) could have been brought about by other causes as well, and consequently their production did not require the will of a rational being, in which, however, the highest and unconditioned good can alone be found. Therefore nothing but the *idea of the law* in itself, *which admittedly is present only in a rational* 16 *being*—so far as it, and not an expected result, is the ground determining the will—can constitute that pre-eminent good which we call moral, a good which is already present in the person acting on this idea and has not to be awaited merely from the result.**

[The categorical imperative.]

But what kind of law can this be the thought of which, even 402]17 without regard to the results expected from it, has to determine the will if this is to be called good absolutely and without qualifi-

---

*A *maxim* is the subjective principle of a volition: an objective principle (that 15 is, one which would also serve subjectively as a practical principle for all rational beings if reason had full control over the faculty of desire) is a practical *law*.

**It might be urged against me that I have merely tried, under cover of the word 16 '*reverence*', to take refuge in an obscure feeling instead of giving a clearly articulated answer to the question by means of a concept of reason. Yet although reverence is a feeling, it is not a feeling *received* through outside influence, but one *self-produced* by a rational concept, and therefore specifically distinct from feelings of the first kind, all of which can be reduced to inclination or fear. What I recognize immediately as law for me, I recognize with reverence, which means merely consciousness of the *subordination* of my will to a law without the mediation of external influences on my senses. Immediate determination of the will by the law and consciousness of this determination is called '*reverence*', so that reverence is regarded as the *effect* of the law on the subject and not as the *cause* of the law. Reverence is properly awareness of a value which demolishes my self-love. Hence there is something which is regarded neither as an object of inclination nor as an object of fear, though it has at the same time some analogy with both. The *object* of reverence is the *law* alone—that law which we impose *on ourselves* but yet as necessary in itself. Considered as a law, we are subject to it without any consultation of self-love; considered as self-imposed it is a consequence of our will. In the first respect it[1] is analogous to fear, in the second to inclination. All reverence for a person is properly only 17 reverence for the law (of honesty and so on) of which that person gives us an example. Because we regard the development of our talents as a duty,[1] we see too in a man of talent a sort of *example of the law* (the law of becoming like him by practice), and this is what constitutes our reverence for him. All moral *interest*, so-called, consists solely in *reverence* for the law.

cation? Since I have robbed the will of every inducement that might arise for it as a consequence of obeying any particular law, nothing is left but the conformity of actions to universal law as such, and this alone must serve the will as its principle. That is to say, I ought never to act except in such a way *that I can also will that my maxim should become a universal law.* Here bare conformity to universal law as such (without having as its base any law prescribing particular actions) is what serves the will as its principle, and must so serve it if duty is not to be everywhere an empty delusion and a chimerical concept. The ordinary reason of mankind also agrees with this completely in its practical judgements and always has the aforesaid principle before its eyes.

18   Take this question, for example. May I not, when I am hard pressed, make a promise with the intention of not keeping it? Here I readily distinguish the two senses which the question can have—Is it prudent, or is it right, to make a false promise? The first no doubt can often be the case. I do indeed see that it is not enough for me to extricate myself from present embarrassment by this subterfuge: I have to consider whether from this lie there may not subsequently accrue to me much greater inconvenience than that from which I now escape, and also—since, with all my supposed *astuteness*, to foresee the consequences is not so easy that I can be sure there is no chance, once confidence in me is lost, of this proving far more disadvantageous than all the ills I now think to avoid—whether it may not be a *more prudent* action to proceed here on a general maxim and make it my habit not to give a promise except with the intention of keeping it. Yet it becomes clear to me at once that such a maxim is always founded solely on fear of consequences. To tell the truth for the sake of duty is something entirely different from doing so out of concern for inconvenient results; for in the first case the concept of the action already contains in itself a law for me, while in the second case I have first of all to look around elsewhere in order to see 19 what effects may be bound up with it for me. When I deviate from 403 the principle of duty, this is quite certainly bad; but if I desert my prudential maxim, this can often be greatly to my advantage, though it is admittedly safer to stick to it. Suppose I seek, however, to learn in the quickest way and yet unerringly how to solve the problem 'Does a lying promise accord with duty?' I have then

to ask myself 'Should I really be content that my maxim (the maxim of getting out of a difficulty by a false promise) should hold as a universal law (one valid both for myself and others)? And could I really say to myself that every one may make a false promise if he finds himself in a difficulty from which he can extricate himself in no other way?' I then become aware at once that I can indeed will to lie, but I can by no means will a universal law of lying; for by such a law there could properly be no promises at all, since it would be futile to profess a will for future action to others who would not believe my profession or who, if they did so over-hastily, would pay me back in like coin;[1] and consequently my maxim, as soon as it was made a universal law, would be bound to annul itself.

Thus I need no far-reaching ingenuity to find out what I have to do in order to possess a good will. Inexperienced in the course 20 of world affairs and incapable of being prepared for all the chances that happen in it, I ask myself only 'Can you also will that your maxim should become a universal law?' Where you cannot, it is to be rejected, and that not because of a prospective loss to you or even to others, but because it cannot fit as a principle into a possible enactment of universal law. For such an enactment reason compels my immediate reverence, into whose grounds (which the philosopher may investigate) I have as yet no *insight*,[1] although I do at least understand this much: reverence is the assessment of a worth which far outweighs all the worth of what is commended by inclination, and the necessity for me to act out of *pure* reverence for the practical law is what constitutes duty, to which every other motive must give way because it is the condition of a will good *in itself*, whose value is above all else.

[Ordinary practical reason.]

In studying the moral knowledge of ordinary human reason we have now arrived at its first principle. This principle it admittedly does not conceive thus abstractly in its universal form; but it does always have it actually before its eyes and does use it as a norm of judgement. It would be easy to show here how human 404 reason, with this compass in hand, is well able to distinguish, in 21 all cases that present themselves, what is good or evil, right or

wrong—provided that, without the least attempt to teach it any-thing new, we merely make reason attend, as Socrates did, to its own principle; and how in consequence there is no need of science or philosophy for knowing what man has to do in order to be honest and good, and indeed to be wise and virtuous. It might even be surmised in advance that acquaintance with what every man is obliged to do, and so also to know, will be the affair of every man, even the most ordinary. Yet we cannot observe without admiration the great advantage which the power of practical judgement has over that of theoretical in the minds of ordinary men. In theoretical judgements, when ordinary reason ventures to depart from the laws of experience and the perceptions of sense, it falls into sheer unintelligibility and self-contradiction, or at least into a chaos of uncertainty, obscurity, and vacillation. On the practical side, however, the power of judgement first begins to show what advantages it has in itself when the ordinary mind excludes all sensuous motives from its practical laws. Then ordinary intelligence becomes even subtle—it may be in juggling with conscience or with other claims as to what is to be called
22 right, or in trying to determine honestly for its own instruction the value of various actions; and, what is most important, it can in the latter case have as good hope of hitting the mark as any that a philosopher can promise himself. Indeed it is almost surer in this than even a philosopher, because he can have no principle different from that of ordinary intelligence, but may easily confuse his judgement with a mass of alien and irrelevant considerations and cause it to swerve from the straight path. Might it not then be more advisable in moral questions to abide by the judgement of ordinary reason and, at the most, to bring in philosophy only in order to set forth the system of morals more fully and intelligibly and to present its rules in a form more convenient for use (though still more so for disputation)—but not in order to lead ordinary human intelligence away from its happy simplicity in respect of action and to set it by means of philosophy on a new path of enquiry and instruction?

[*The need for philosophy.*]

Innocence is a splendid thing, only it has the misfortune not
405 to keep very well and to be easily misled. On this account even

wisdom—which in itself consists more in doing and not doing than in knowing—does require science as well, not in order to learn from it, but in order to win acceptance and durability for its own 23 prescriptions. Man feels in himself a powerful counterweight to all the commands of duty presented to him by reason as so worthy of esteem—the counterweight of his needs and inclinations, whose total satisfaction he grasps under the name of 'happiness'. But reason, without promising anything to inclination, enjoins its commands relentlessly, and therefore, so to speak, with disregard and neglect of these turbulent and seemingly equitable claims (which refuse to be suppressed by any command). From this there arises a *natural dialectic*—that is, a disposition to quibble with these strict laws of duty, to throw doubt on their validity or at least on their purity and strictness, and to make them, where possible, more adapted to our wishes and inclinations; that is, to pervert their very foundations and destroy their whole dignity—a result which in the end even ordinary human reason is unable to approve.

In this way the *common reason of mankind* is impelled, not by any need for speculation (which never assails it so long as it is content to be mere sound reason), but on practical grounds themselves, to leave its own sphere and take a step into the field of *practical philosophy*. It there seeks to acquire information and precise instruc- 24 tion about the source of its own principle, and about the correct function of this principle in comparison with maxims based on need and inclination, in order that it may escape from the embarrassment of antagonistic claims and may avoid the risk of losing all genuine moral principles because of the ambiguity into which it easily falls. Thus ordinary reason, when cultivated in its practical use, gives rise insensibly to a *dialectic* which constrains it to seek help in philosophy, just as happens in its theoretical use; and consequently in the first case as little as in the second will it anywhere else than in a full critique of our reason be able to find peace.

PASSAGE FROM POPULAR MORAL PHILOSOPHY
TO A METAPHYSIC OF MORALS

[The use of examples.]

If so far we have drawn our concept of duty from the ordinary use of our practical reason, it must by no means be inferred that we have treated it as a concept of experience. On the contrary, when we pay attention to our experience of human conduct, we meet frequent and—as we ourselves admit—justified complaints that we can adduce no certain examples of the spirit which acts out of pure duty, and that, although much may be done *in accordance with* the commands of *duty*, it remains doubtful whether it really is done *for the sake of duty* and so has a moral value. Hence at all times there have been philosophers who have absolutely denied the presence of this spirit in human. actions and have ascribed everything to a more or less refined self-love. Yet they have not cast doubt on the rightness of the concept of morality. They have spoken rather with deep regret of the frailty and impurity of human nature, which is on their view noble enough
26 to take as its rule an Idea so worthy of reverence, but at the same time too weak to follow it: the reason which should serve it for making laws it uses only to look after the interest of inclinations, whether singly or—at the best—in their greatest mutual compatibility.

407   In actual fact it is absolutely impossible for experience to establish with complete certainty a single case in which the maxim of an action in other respects right has rested solely on moral grounds and on the thought of one's duty. It is indeed at times the case that after the keenest self-examination we find nothing that without the moral motive of duty could have been strong enough to move us to this or that good action and to so great a sacrifice; but we cannot infer from this with certainty that it is not some secret impulse of self-love which has actually, under

the mere show of the Idea of duty, been the cause genuinely determining our will. We are pleased to flatter ourselves with the false claim to a nobler motive, but in fact we can never, even by the most strenuous self-examination, get to the bottom of our secret impulses; for when moral value is in question, we are concerned, not with the actions which we see, but with their inner principles, which we cannot see.

Furthermore, to those who deride all morality as the mere 27 phantom of a human imagination which gets above itself out of vanity we can do no service more pleasing than to admit that the concepts of duty must be drawn solely from experience (just as out of slackness we willingly persuade ourselves that this is so in the case of all other concepts); for by so doing we prepare for them an assured triumph. Out of love for humanity I am willing to allow that most of our actions may accord with duty; but if we look more closely at our scheming and striving, we everywhere come across the dear self, which is always turning up; and it is on this that the purpose of our actions is based—not on the strict command of duty, which would often require self-denial. One need not be exactly a foe to virtue, but merely a dispassionate observer declining to take the liveliest wish for goodness straight away as its realization, in order at certain moments (particularly with advancing years and with a power of judgement at once made shrewder by experience and also more keen in observation) to become doubtful whether any genuine virtue is actually to be encountered in the world. And then nothing can protect us against a complete falling away from our Ideas of duty, or can preserve in the soul a grounded reverence for its law, except the clear conviction that even if there never have been actions springing from such pure sources, the question at issue here is not whether 408] 28 this or that has happened; that, on the contrary, reason by itself and independently of all appearances commands what ought to happen; that consequently actions of which the world has perhaps hitherto given no example—actions whose practicability might well be doubted by those who rest everything on experience— are nevertheless commanded unrelentingly by reason; and that, for instance, although up to now there may have existed no loyal friend, pure loyalty in friendship can be no less required from every man, inasmuch as this duty, prior to all experience, is contained as duty in general[1] in the Idea of a reason which determines the will by *a priori* grounds.

It may be added that unless we wish to deny to the concept of morality all truth and all relation to a possible object, we cannot dispute that its law is of such widespread significance as to hold, not merely for men, but for all *rational beings as such*—not merely subject to contingent conditions and exceptions, but *with absolute necessity*.[2] It is therefore clear that no experience can give us occasion to infer even the possibility of such apodeictic laws. For 29 by what right can we make what is perhaps valid only under the contingent conditions of humanity into an object of unlimited reverence as a universal precept for every rational nature? And how could laws for determining *our* will be taken as laws for determining the will of a rational being as such—and only because of this for determining ours—if these laws were merely empirical and did not have their source completely *a priori* in pure, but practical, reason?

What is more, we cannot do morality a worse service than by seeking to derive it from examples. Every example of it presented to me must first itself be judged by moral principles in order to decide if it is fit to serve as an original example—that is, as a model: it can in no way supply the prime source for the concept of morality. Even the Holy One of the gospel must first be compared with our ideal of moral perfection before we can recognize him to be such. He also says of himself: 'Why callest thou me (whom thou seest) good? There is none good (the archetype of the good) but one, that is, God (whom thou seest not)'. But where do we 409 get the concept of God as the highest good? Solely from the *Idea* of moral perfection,[1] which reason traces *a priori* and conjoins inseparably with the concept of a free will. Imitation has no place 30 in morality, and examples serve us only for encouragement—that is, they set beyond doubt the practicability of what the law commands; they make perceptible what the practical law expresses more generally; but they can never entitle us to set aside their true original, which resides in reason, and to model ourselves upon examples.

[*Popular philosophy*.]

If there can be no genuine supreme principle of morality which is not grounded on pure reason alone independently of

all experience, it should be unnecessary, I think, even to raise
the question whether it is a good thing to set forth in general
(*in abstracto*) these concepts which hold *a priori*, together with
their corresponding principles, so far as our knowledge is to be
distinguished from ordinary knowledge and described as philosophical. Yet in our days it may well be necessary to do so. For
if we took a vote on which is to be preferred, pure rational
knowledge detached from everything empirical—that is to say, a
metaphysic of morals—or popular practical philosophy, we can
guess at once on which side the preponderance would fall.

It is certainly most praiseworthy to come down to the level
of popular thought when we have previously risen to the principles
of pure reason and are fully satisfied of our success. This
could be described as first *grounding* moral philosophy on meta- 31
physics[1] and subsequently winning *acceptance* for it by giving it
a popular character after it has been established. But it is utterly
senseless to aim at popularity in our first enquiry, upon which
the whole correctness of our principles depends. It is not merely
that such a procedure can never lay claim to the extremely rare
merit of a truly *philosophical popularity*, since we require no skill
to make ourselves intelligible to the multitude once we renounce
all profundity of thought: what it turns out is a disgusting hotch-
potch of second-hand observations and semi-rational principles on
which the empty-headed regale themselves, because this is something that can be used in the chit-chat of daily life. Men of insight,
on the other hand, feel confused by it and avert their eyes with
a dissatisfaction which, however, they are unable to cure. Yet
philosophers, who can perfectly well see through this deception,
get little hearing when they summon us for a time from this 410
would-be popularity in order that they may win the right to be
genuinely popular only after definite insight has been attained.

We need only look at the attempts to deal with morality in
this favoured style. What we shall encounter in an amazing medley
is at one time the particular character of human nature (but along
with this also the Idea of a rational nature as such), at another
perfection, at another happiness; here moral feeling and there the 32
fear of God; something of this and also something of that. But
it never occurs to these writers to ask whether the principles of
morality are to be sought at all in our acquaintance with human

nature (which we can get only from experience); nor does it occur to them that if this is not so—if these principles are to be found completely *a priori* and free from empirical elements in the concepts of pure reason and absolutely nowhere else even to the slightest extent—they had better adopt the plan of separating off this enquiry altogether as pure practical philosophy or (if one may use a name so much decried) as a metaphysic* of morals; of bringing this to full completeness entirely by itself; and of bidding the public which demands popularity to await in hope the outcome of this undertaking.

Nevertheless such a completely isolated metaphysic of morals,
33 mixed with no anthropology, no theology, no physics or hyperphysics, still less with occult qualities (which might be called hypophysical), is not only an indispensable substratum of all theoretical and precisely defined knowledge of duties, but is at the same time a desideratum of the utmost importance for the actual execution of moral precepts. Unmixed with the alien element of added empirical inducements, the pure thought of duty, and in general of the moral law, has by way of reason alone (which first learns from this that by itself it is able to be practical as well as theoretical) an influence on the human heart so much
411 more powerful than all the further impulses** capable of being called up from the field of experience that in the consciousness of its own dignity[1] reason despises these impulses and is able

32   *We can, if we like, distinguish pure moral philosophy (metaphysics) from applied (applied, that is, to human nature)—just as pure mathematics is distinguished from applied mathematics and pure logic from applied logic. By this terminology we are at once reminded that moral principles are not grounded on the peculiarities of human nature, but must be established *a priori* by themselves; and yet that from such principles it must be possible to derive practical rules for human nature as well, just as it is for every kind of rational nature.

33   **I have a letter from the late distinguished Professor *Sulzer*,[1] in which he asks me what it is that makes moral instruction so ineffective, however convincing it may be in the eyes of reason. Because of my efforts to make it complete, my answer came too late. Yet it is just this: the teachers themselves do not make their concepts pure, but—since they try to do too well by hunting everywhere for inducements to be moral—they spoil their medicine altogether by their very attempt to make it really powerful. For the most ordinary observation shows that when
34 a righteous act is represented as being done with a steadfast mind in complete disregard of any advantage in this or in another world, and even under the greatest temptations of affliction or allurement, it leaves far behind it any similar action affected even in the slightest degree by an alien impulse and casts it into the shade: it uplifts the soul and rouses a wish that we too could act in this way. Even children of moderate age feel this impression, and duties should never be presented to them in any other way.

gradually to become their master. In place of this, a mixed moral philosophy, compounded of impulsions from feeling and inclination and at the same time of rational concepts, must make the 34 mind waver between motives which can be brought under no single principle and which can guide us only by mere accident to the good, but very often also to the evil.

[Review of conclusions.]

From these considerations the following conclusions emerge. All moral concepts have their seat and origin in reason completely *a priori*, and indeed in the most ordinary human reason just as much as in the most highly speculative: they cannot be abstracted from any empirical, and therefore merely contingent, knowledge. In this purity of their origin is to be found their very worthiness to serve as supreme practical principles, and everything empirical added to them is just so much taken away from their genuine influence and from the absolute value of the corresponding actions.[1] It is not only a requirement of the utmost necessity in respect of theory, where our concern is solely with speculation, but is also 35 of the utmost practical importance, to draw these concepts and laws from pure reason, to set them forth pure and unmixed, and indeed to determine the extent of this whole practical, but pure, rational knowledge—that is, to determine the whole power of pure practical reason. We ought never—as speculative philosophy[1] does allow and even at times finds necessary—to make principles depend on the special nature of human reason. Since moral laws have to 412 hold for every rational being as such, we ought rather to derive our principles from the general concept of a rational being as such,[2] and on this basis to expound the whole of ethics—which requires anthropology for its *application* to man—at first independently as pure philosophy, that is, entirely as metaphysics[3] (which we can very well do in this wholly abstract kind of knowledge). We know well that without possessing such a metaphysics it is a futile endeavour, I will not say to determine accurately for speculative judgement the moral element of duty in all that accords with duty—but that it is impossible, even in ordinary and practical usage, particularly in that of moral instruction, to base morals on their genuine principles and so to bring about pure moral dispositions and engraft them on men's minds for the highest good of the world.

36   In this task of ours we have to progress by natural stages, not merely from ordinary moral judgement (which is here worthy of great respect) to philosophical judgement, as we have already done,[1] but from popular philosophy, which goes no further than it can get by fumbling about with the aid of examples, to metaphysics. (This no longer lets itself be held back by anything empirical, and indeed—since it must survey the complete totality[2] of this kind of knowledge—goes right to Ideas, where examples themselves fail.) For this purpose we must follow—and must portray in detail —the power of practical reason from the general rules determining it right up to the point where there springs from it the concept of duty.[3]

[*Imperatives in general.*]

Everything in nature works in accordance with laws. Only a rational being has the power to act *in accordance with his idea* of laws—that is, in accordance with principles—and only so has he a *will*. Since *reason* is required in order to derive actions from laws,[4] the will is nothing but practical reason. If reason infallibly determines the will, then in a being of this kind the actions which are recognized to be objectively necessary are also subjectively necessary—that is to say, the will is then a power to choose *only that* which reason independently of inclination recognizes to be 37 practically necessary, that is, to be good. But if reason solely by itself is not sufficient to determine the will; if the will is exposed also to subjective conditions (certain impulsions) which do not always harmonize with the objective ones; if, in a word, the will 413 is not *in itself* completely in accord with reason (as actually happens in the case of men); then actions which are recognized to be objectively necessary are subjectively contingent, and the determining of such a will in accordance with objective laws is *necessitation*. That is to say, the relation of objective laws to a will not good through and through is conceived as one in which the will of a rational being, although it is determined[1] by principles of reason, does not necessarily follow these principles in virtue of its own nature.

The conception of an objective principle so far as this principle is necessitating for a will is called a command (of reason), and the formula of this command is called an *Imperative*.

All imperatives are expressed by an *'ought'* (*Sollen*). By this they mark the relation of an objective law of reason to a will which is not necessarily determined by this law in virtue of its subjective constitution (the relation of necessitation). They say that something would be good to do or to leave undone; only they say it to a will which does not always do a thing because 38 it has been informed that this is a good thing to do. The practically *good* is that which determines the will by concepts of reason, and therefore not by subjective causes, but objectively—that is, on grounds valid for every rational being as such. It is distinguished from the *pleasant* as that which influences the will, not as a principle of reason valid for every one, but solely through the medium of sensation by purely subjective causes valid only for the senses of this person or that.★

A perfectly good will would thus stand quite as much under 414] 39 objective laws (laws of the good), but it could not on this account be conceived as *necessitated* to act in conformity with law, since of itself, in accordance with its subjective constitution, it can be determined only by the concept of the good. Hence for the *divine* will, and in general for a *holy* will, there are no imperatives: '*I ought*' is here out of place, because '*I will*' is already of itself necessarily in harmony with the law. Imperatives are in consequence only formulae for expressing the relation of objective laws of willing to the subjective imperfection of the will of this or that rational being—for example, of the human will.

★The dependence of the power of appetition on sensations is called an inclination, 38 and thus an inclination always indicates a *need*. The dependence of a contingently determinable will on principles of reason is called an *interest*. Hence an interest is found only where there is a dependent will which in itself is not always in accord with reason: to a divine will we cannot ascribe any interest. But even the human will can *take an interest* in something without therefore *acting from interest*. The first expression signifies *practical* interest in the action; the second *pathological* interest in the object of the action. The first indicates only dependence of the will on principles of reason by itself; the second its dependence on principles of reason at the service of inclination—that is to say, where reason merely supplies a practical rule for meeting the need of inclination.[1] In the first case what interests me is the action; in the second case what interests me is the object of the action (so far as this object is pleasant to me). We have seen in Chapter I that in an action done for the sake of duty we must have regard, not to interest in the object, but to interest in the action itself and in its rational principle (namely, the law).

[*Classification of imperatives.*]

All *imperatives* command either *hypothetically* or *categorically*. Hypothetical imperatives declare a possible action to be practically necessary as a means to the attainment of something else that one wills (or that one may will). A categorical imperative would be one which represented an action as objectively necessary in itself apart from its relation to a further end.

Every practical law represents a possible action as good and therefore as necessary for a subject whose actions are determined 40 by reason. Hence all imperatives are formulae for determining an action which is necessary in accordance with the principle of a will in some sense good. If the action would be good solely as a means *to something else*, the imperative is *hypothetical*; if the action is represented as good *in itself* and therefore as necessary, in virtue of its[1] principle, for a will which of itself accords with reason, then the imperative is *categorical*.

An imperative therefore tells me which of my possible actions would be good; and it formulates a practical rule for a will that does not perform an action straight away because the action is good—whether because the subject does not always know that it is good or because, even if he did know this, he might still act on maxims contrary to the objective principles of practical reason.

A hypothetical imperative thus says only that an action is good for some purpose or other, either *possible* or *actual*. In the 415 first case it is a *problematic* practical principle; in the second case an *assertoric* practical principle. A categorical imperative, which declares an action to be objectively necessary in itself without reference to some purpose—that is, even without any further end—ranks as an *apodeictic* practical principle.

41 Everything that is possible only through the efforts of some rational being can be conceived as a possible purpose of some will; and consequently there are in fact innumerable principles of action so far as action is thought necessary in order to achieve some possible purpose which can be effected by it. All sciences have a practical part consisting of problems which suppose that some end is possible for us and of imperatives which tell us how it is to be attained. Hence the latter can in general be called imperatives of *skill*. Here there is absolutely no question about the rationality

or goodness of the end, but only about what must be done to attain it. A prescription required by a doctor in order to cure his man completely and one required by a poisoner in order to make sure of killing him are of equal value so far as each serves to effect its purpose perfectly. Since in early youth we do not know what ends may present themselves to us in the course of life, parents seek above all to make their children learn things *of many kinds*; they provide carefully for *skill* in the use of means to all sorts of *arbitrary* ends, of none of which can they be certain that it could not[1] in the future become an actual purpose of their ward, while it is always *possible* that he might adopt it. Their care in this matter is so great that they commonly neglect on this account to form and correct the judgement of their children about the worth of the things which they might possibly adopt as ends.   42

There is, however, *one* end that can be presupposed as actual in all rational beings (so far as they are dependent beings to whom imperatives apply); and thus there is one purpose which they not only *can* have, but which we can assume with certainty that they all *do* have by a natural necessity—the purpose, namely, of *happiness*. A hypothetical imperative which affirms the practical necessity of an action as a means to the furtherance of happiness is *assertoric*. We may represent it, not simply as necessary to an uncertain, merely possible purpose, but as necessary to a purpose which we can presuppose *a priori* and with certainty to be present in every man because it belongs to his very being. Now skill in the choice 416 of means to one's own greatest well-being can be called *prudence** in the narrowest sense.[1] Thus an imperative concerned with the choice of means to one's own happiness—that is, a precept of 43 prudence—still remains *hypothetical*: an action is commanded, not absolutely, but only as a means to a further purpose.

Finally, there is an imperative which, without being based on, and conditioned by, any further purpose to be attained by a certain line of conduct, enjoins this conduct immediately. This imperative

---

*The word 'prudence' (*Klugheit*) is used in a double sense: in one sense it can 42 have the name of 'worldly wisdom' (*Weltklugheit*); in a second sense that of 'personal wisdom' (*Privatklugheit*). The first is the skill of a man in influencing others in order to use them for his own ends. The second is sagacity in combining all these ends to his own lasting advantage.[1] The latter is properly that to which the value of the former can itself be traced; and of him who is prudent in the first sense, but not in the second, we might better say that he is clever and astute, but on the whole imprudent.

is *categorical*. It is concerned, not with the matter of the action and its presumed results, but with its form and with the principle from which it follows; and what is essentially good in the action consists in the mental disposition, let the consequences be what they may. This imperative may be called the imperative of *morality*.

Willing in accordance with these three kinds of principle is also sharply distinguished by a *dissimilarity* in the necessitation of the will. To make this dissimilarity obvious we should, I think, name these kinds of principle most appropriately in their order if we said they were either *rules* of skill or *counsels* of prudence or *commands* (*laws*) of morality. For only *law* carries with it the concept of an *unconditioned*, and yet objective and so universally 44 valid, *necessity*; and commands are laws which must be obeyed— that is, must be followed even against inclination. *Counsel* does indeed involve necessity, but necessity valid only under a subjective and contingent condition—namely, if this or that man counts this or that as belonging to his happiness. As against this, a categorical imperative is limited by no condition and can quite precisely be called a command, as being absolutely, although practically,[1] necessary. We could also call imperatives of the first kind *technical* 417 (concerned with art); of the second kind *pragmatic** (concerned with well-being); of the third kind *moral* (concerned with free conduct as such[2]—that is, with morals).

[*How are imperatives possible?*]

The question now arises 'How are all these imperatives possible?' This question does not ask how we can conceive the execution of an action commanded by the imperative, but merely how we can conceive the necessitation of the will expressed by the imperative in setting us a task.[3] How an imperative of skill is possible requires no special discussion. Who wills the end, wills 45 (so far as reason has decisive influence on his actions) also the means

44   *It seems to me that the proper meaning of the word '*pragmatic*' can be defined most accurately in this way. For those *Sanctions* are called Pragmatic which, properly speaking, do not spring as necessary laws from the Natural Right of States, but from *forethought* in regard to the general welfare.[1] A *history* is written pragmatically when it teaches *prudence*—that is, when it instructs the world of to-day how to provide for its own advantage better than, or at least as well as, the world of other times.

which are indispensably necessary and in his power. So far as willing is concerned, this proposition is analytic: for in my willing of an object as an effect there is already conceived[1] the causality of myself as an acting cause—that is, the use of means; and from the concept of willing an end the imperative merely extracts the concept of actions necessary to this end. (Synthetic propositions are required in order to determine the means to a proposed end, but these are concerned, not with the reason for performing the act of will, but with the cause which produces the object.) That in order to divide a line into two equal parts on a sure principle I must from its ends describe two intersecting arcs—this is admittedly taught by mathematics only in synthetic propositions; but when I know that the aforesaid effect can be produced only by such an action, the proposition 'If I fully will the effect, I also will the action required for it' is analytic; for it is one and the same thing to conceive something as an effect possible in a certain way through me and to conceive myself as acting in the same way with respect to it.

If it were only as easy to find a determinate concept of happiness, the imperatives of prudence would agree entirely with those of skill and would be equally analytic. For here as there it could alike be said 'Who wills the end, wills also (necessarily, if he accords with reason) the sole means which are in his power'. Unfortunately, however, the concept of happiness is so indeterminate a concept that although every man wants to attain happiness, he can never say definitely and in unison with himself what it really is that he wants and wills. The reason for this is that all the elements which belong to the concept of happiness are without exception empirical—that is, they must be borrowed from experience; but that none the less there is required for the Idea of happiness an absolute whole, a maximum of well-being in my present, and in every future, state. Now it is impossible for the most intelligent, and at the same time most powerful, but nevertheless finite, being to form here a determinate concept of what he really wills. Is it riches that he wants? How much anxiety, envy, and pestering might he not bring in this way on his own head! Is it knowledge and insight? This might perhaps merely give him an eye so sharp that it would make evils at present hidden from him and yet unavoidable seem all the more frightful, or

would add a load of still further needs to the desires which already
47 give him trouble enough. Is it long life? Who will guarantee that
it would not be a long misery? Is it at least health? How often
has infirmity of body kept a man from excesses into which perfect
health would have let him fall!—and so on. In short, he has no
principle by which he is able to decide with complete certainty
what will make him truly happy, since for this he would require
omniscience. Thus we cannot act on determinate principles in
order to be happy, but only on empirical counsels, for example,
of diet, frugality, politeness, reserve, and so on—things which
experience shows contribute most to well-being on the average.
From this it follows that imperatives of prudence, speaking strictly,
do not command at all—that is, cannot exhibit actions objectively
as practically *necessary*; that they are rather to be taken as recom-
mendations (*consilia*), than as commands (*praecepta*), of reason; that
the problem of determining certainly and universally what action
will promote the happiness of a rational being is completely
insoluble; and consequently that in regard to this there is no imperative possible which in the strictest sense could command us to do
what will make us happy, since happiness is an Ideal, not of reason,
but of imagination—an Ideal resting merely on empirical grounds,
419 of which it is vain to expect that they should determine an action
48 by which we could attain the totality of a series of consequences
which is in fact infinite. Nevertheless, if we assume that the means
to happiness could be discovered with certainty, this imperative
of prudence would be an analytic practical proposition; for it
differs from the imperative of skill only in this—that in the latter
the end is merely possible, while in the former the end is given.
In spite of this difference, since both command solely the means
to something assumed to be willed as an end, the imperative which
commands him who wills the end to will the means is in both
cases analytic. Thus there is likewise no difficulty in regard to the
possibility of an imperative of prudence.

Beyond all doubt, the question 'How is the imperative of *morality*
possible?' is the only one in need of a solution; for it is in no way
hypothetical, and consequently we cannot base the objective
necessity which it affirms on any presupposition, as we can with
hypothetical imperatives. Only we must never forget here that it
is impossible to settle *by an example*, and so empirically, whether

there is any imperative of this kind at all: we must rather suspect that all imperatives which seem to be categorical may none the less be covertly hypothetical. Take, for example, the saying 'Thou shalt make no false promises'. Let us assume that the necessity for this abstention is no mere advice for the avoidance of some further 49 evil—as it might be said 'You ought not to make a lying promise lest, when this comes to light, you destroy your credit'. Let us hold, on the contrary, that an action of this kind must be considered as bad in itself, and that the imperative of prohibition is therefore categorical. Even so, we cannot with any certainty show by an example that the will is determined here solely by the law without any further motive, although it may appear to be so; for it is always possible that fear of disgrace, perhaps also hidden dread of other risks, may unconsciously influence the will. Who can prove by experience that a cause is not present? Experience shows only that it is not perceived. In such a case, however, the so-called moral imperative, which as such appears to be categorical and unconditioned, would in fact be only a pragmatic prescription calling attention to our advantage and merely bidding us take this into account.

We shall thus have to investigate the possibility of a *categorical* imperative entirely *a priori*, since here we do not enjoy the advantage 420 of having its reality given in experience and so of being obliged merely to explain, and not to establish, its possibility.[1] So much, however, can be seen provisionally—that the categorical imperative alone purports to be a practical *law*, while all the rest may be 50 called *principles* of the will but not laws; for an action necessary merely in order to achieve an arbitrary purpose can be considered as in itself contingent, and we can always escape from the precept if we abandon the purpose; whereas an unconditioned command does not leave it open to the will to do the opposite at its discretion and therefore alone carries with it that necessity which we demand from a law.

In the second place, with this categorical imperative or law of morality the reason for our difficulty (in comprehending its possibility) is a very serious one. We have here a synthetic *a priori* practical proposition;* and since in theoretical knowledge there is

*Without presupposing a condition taken from some inclination I connect an 50 action with the will *a priori* and therefore necessarily (although only objectively so —that is, only subject to the Idea of a reason having full power over all subjective

so much difficulty in comprehending the possibility of propositions of this kind, it may readily be gathered that in practical knowledge the difficulty will be no less.

[The Formula of Universal Law.]

51   In this task we wish first to enquire whether perhaps the mere concept of a categorical imperative may not also provide us with the formula containing the only proposition that can be a categorical imperative; for even when we know the purport of such an absolute command, the question of its possibility will still require a special and troublesome effort, which we postpone to the final chapter.

When I conceive a *hypothetical* imperative in general, I do not know beforehand what it will contain—until its condition is given. But if I conceive a *categorical* imperative, I know at once what it contains. For since besides the law this imperative contains only
421 the necessity that our maxim* should conform[1] to this law, while the law, as we have seen, contains no condition to limit it, there remains nothing over to which the maxim has to conform except
52 the universality of a law as such; and it is this conformity alone that the imperative properly asserts to be necessary.

There is therefore only a single categorical imperative and it is this: '*Act only on that maxim through*[1] *which you can at the same time will that it should become a universal law*'.

Now if all imperatives of duty can be derived from this one imperative as their principle, then even although we leave it unsettled whether what we call duty may not be an empty concept, we shall still be able to show at least what we understand by it and what the concept means.

---

impulses to action). Here we have a practical proposition in which the willing of an action is not derived analytically from some other willing already presupposed[1] (for we do not possess any such perfect will[2]), but is on the contrary connected immediately[3] with the concept of the will of a rational being as something which is not contained in this concept.

51   *A *maxim* is a subjective principle of action and must be distinguished from an *objective principle*—namely, a practical law. The former contains a practical rule determined by reason in accordance with the conditions of the subject (often his ignorance or again his inclinations): it is thus a principle on which the subject *acts*. A law, on the other hand, is an objective principle valid for every rational being; and it is a principle on which he *ought to act*—that is, an imperative.[1]

[*The Formula of the Law of Nature.*]

Since the universality of the law governing the production of effects constitutes what is properly called *nature* in its most general sense (nature as regards its form)² —that is, the existence of things so far as determined by universal laws—the universal imperative of duty may also run as follows: '*Act as if the maxim of your action were to become through your will a universal law of nature.*'

[*Illustrations.*]

We will now enumerate a few duties, following their customary division into duties towards self and duties towards others and into 53 perfect and imperfect duties.*

1. A man feels sick of life as the result of a series of misfortunes that has mounted to the point of despair, but he is still so far in 422 possession of his reason as to ask himself whether taking his own life may not be contrary to his duty to himself. He now applies the test 'Can the maxim of my action really become a universal law of nature?' His maxim is 'From self-love I make it my principle to shorten my life if its continuance threatens more evil than it promises pleasure'. The only further question to ask is whether this principle of self-love can become a universal law of nature. It is then seen at once that a system of nature by whose law the very same feeling whose function (*Bestimmung*) is to stimulate the 54 furtherance of life should actually destroy life would contradict itself and consequently could not subsist as a system of nature.¹ Hence this maxim cannot possibly hold as a universal law of nature and is therefore entirely opposed to the supreme principle of all duty.

2. Another finds himself driven to borrowing money because of need. He well knows that he will not be able to pay it back; but he sees too that he will get no loan unless he gives a firm promise to pay it back within a fixed time. He is inclined to make such a promise; but he has still enough conscience to ask 'Is it not

*It should be noted that I reserve my division of duties entirely for a future 53 *Metaphysic of Morals* and that my present division is therefore put forward as arbitrary (merely for the purpose of arranging my examples). Further, I understand here by a perfect duty one which allows no exception in the interests of inclination,¹ and so I recognize among *perfect duties*, not only outer ones, but also inner.² This is contrary to the accepted usage of the schools, but I do not intend to justify it here, since for my purpose it is all one whether this point is conceded or not.

unlawful and contrary to duty to get out of difficulties in this way?' Supposing, however, he did resolve to do so, the maxim of his action would run thus: 'Whenever I believe myself short of money, I will borrow money and promise to pay it back, though I know that this will never be done'. Now this principle of self-love or personal advantage is perhaps quite compatible with my own entire future welfare; only there remains the question 'Is it right?' I therefore transform the demand of self-love into a universal law and frame my question thus: 'How would things stand if my maxim became a universal law?' I then see straight away that this maxim can never rank as a universal law of nature 55 and be self-consistent, but must necessarily contradict itself. For the universality of a law that every one believing himself to be in need can make any promise he pleases with the intention not to keep it would make promising, and the very purpose of promising, itself impossible, since no one would believe he was being promised anything, but would laugh at utterances of this kind as empty shams.

3. A third finds in himself a talent whose cultivation would 423 make him a useful man for all sorts of purposes. But he sees himself in comfortable circumstances, and he prefers to give himself up to pleasure rather than to bother about increasing and improving his fortunate natural aptitudes. Yet he asks himself further 'Does my maxim of neglecting my natural gifts, besides agreeing in itself with my tendency to indulgence, agree also with what is called duty?' He then sees that a system of nature could indeed always subsist under such a universal law, although (like the South Sea Islanders) every man should let his talents rust and should be bent on devoting his life solely to idleness, indulgence, procreation, and, in a word, to enjoyment. Only he cannot possibly *will* that this should become a universal law of nature or should be 56 implanted in us as such a law by a natural instinct. For as a rational being he necessarily wills that all his powers should be developed, since they serve him, and are given him, for all sorts of possible ends.

4. Yet a *fourth* is himself flourishing, but he sees others who have to struggle with great hardships (and whom he could easily help); and he thinks 'What does it matter to me? Let every one be as happy as Heaven wills or as he can make himself; I won't deprive

him of anything; I won't even envy him; only I have no wish to contribute anything to his well-being or to his support in distress!' Now admittedly if such an attitude were a universal law of nature, mankind could get on perfectly well—better no doubt than if everybody prates about sympathy and goodwill, and even takes pains, on occasion, to practise them, but on the other hand cheats where he can, traffics in human rights, or violates them in other ways. But although it is possible that a universal law of nature could subsist in harmony with this maxim, yet it is impossible to *will* that such a principle should hold everywhere as a law of nature. For a will which decided in this way would be in conflict with itself, since many a situation might arise in which the man needed love and sympathy from others,[1] and in which, by such a law of nature sprung from his own will, he would rob himself [57] of all hope of the help he wants for himself.

[The canon of moral judgement.]

These are some of the many actual duties—or at least of what we take to be such—whose derivation from the single principle cited above leaps to the eye. We must *be able to will* that a maxim [424] of our action should become a universal law—this is the general canon for all moral judgement of action. Some actions are so constituted that their maxim cannot even be *conceived* as a universal law of nature without contradiction, let alone be *willed* as what *ought* to become one. In the case of others we do not find this inner impossibility, but it is still impossible to *will* that their maxim should be raised to the universality of a law of nature, because such a will would contradict itself. It is easily seen that the first kind of action is opposed to strict or narrow (rigorous) duty, the second only to wider (meritorious) duty;[1] and thus that by these examples all duties—so far as the type of obligation is concerned (not the object of dutiful action)[2]—are fully set out in their dependence on our single principle.

If we now attend to ourselves whenever we transgress a duty, we find that we in fact do not will that our maxim should become [58] a universal law—since this is impossible for us—but rather that its opposite should remain a law universally: we only take the liberty of making an *exception* to it for ourselves (or even just for this once) to the advantage of our inclination. Consequently if we weighed it all up from one and the same point of view—that of reason—we should find a contradiction in our own will, the contradiction that a certain principle should be objectively necessary as a universal law and yet subjectively should not hold universally but should admit of exceptions. Since, however, we first consider our action from the point of view of a will wholly in accord with reason, and then consider precisely the same action from the point of view of a will affected by inclination, there is here actually no contradiction, but rather an opposition of inclination to the precept of reason (*antagonismus*), whereby the universality of the principle (*universalitas*) is turned into a mere generality (*generalitas*) so that the practical principle of reason may meet our maxim half-way. This procedure, though in our own impartial judgement it cannot be justified, proves none the less that we in fact recognize the validity of the categorical imperative and (with all respect for it) merely 59 permit ourselves a few exceptions which are, as we pretend, inconsiderable and apparently forced upon us.

425   We have thus at least shown this much—that if duty is a concept which is to have meaning and real legislative authority for our actions, this can be expressed only in categorical imperatives and by no means in hypothetical ones. At the same time—and this is already a great deal—we have set forth distinctly, and determinately for every type of application, the content of the categorical imperative, which must contain the principle of all duty (if there is to be such a thing at all). But we are still not so far advanced as to prove *a priori* that there actually is an imperative of this kind—that there is a practical law which by itself commands absolutely and without any further motives, and that the following of this law is duty.

[The need for pure ethics.]

For the purpose of achieving this proof it is of the utmost importance to take warning that we should not dream for a moment of trying to derive the reality of this principle from *the special characteristics of human nature*. For duty has to be a practical, unconditioned necessity of action; it must therefore hold for all rational beings (to whom alone an imperative can apply at all), and *only because of this* can it also be a law for all human wills. Whatever, on the other hand, is derived from the special predisposition of humanity, from certain feelings and propensities, 60 and even, if this were possible, from some special bent peculiar to human reason and not holding necessarily for the will of every rational being—all this can indeed supply a personal maxim, but not a law: it can give us a subjective principle—one on which we have a propensity and inclination to act—but not an objective one on which we should be *directed* to act although our every propensity, inclination, and natural bent were opposed to it; so much so that the sublimity and inner worth of the command is the more manifest[1] in a duty, the fewer are the subjective causes for obeying it and the more those against—without, however, on this account weakening in the slightest the necessitation exercised by the law or detracting anything from its validity.

It is here that philosophy is seen in actual fact to be placed in a precarious position, which is supposed to be firm although neither in heaven nor on earth is there anything from which it depends or on which it is based. It is here that she has to show her purity as the authoress of her own laws—not as the mouth-piece of laws whispered to her by some implanted sense or by who knows what tutelary nature, all of which laws together, though they may always be better than nothing, can never furnish 426 us with principles dictated by reason. These principles must have an origin entirely and completely *a priori* and must at the same time derive from this their sovereign authority—that they expect nothing from the inclinations of man, but everything from the 61 supremacy of the law and from the reverence due to it, or in default of this condemn man to self-contempt and inward abhorrence.

Hence everything that is empirical is, as a contribution to the principle of morality,[1] not only wholly unsuitable for the purpose, but is even highly injurious to the purity of morals; for in morals the proper worth of an absolutely good will, a worth elevated above all price, lies precisely in this—that the principle of action is free from all influence by contingent grounds, the only kind that experience can supply. Against the slack, or indeed ignoble, attitude which seeks for the moral principle among empirical motives and laws we cannot give a warning too strongly or too often; for human reason in its weariness is fain to rest upon this pillow and in a dream of sweet illusions (which lead it to embrace a cloud in mistake for Juno)[2] to foist into the place of morality some misbegotten mongrel patched up from limbs of very varied ancestry and looking like anything you please, only not like virtue, to him who has once beheld her in her true shape.*

62   Our question therefore is this: 'Is it a necessary law *for all rational beings* always to judge their actions by reference to those maxims of which they can themselves will that they should serve as universal laws?' If there is such a law, it must already be connected (entirely *a priori*) with the concept of the will of a rational being as such.[1] But in order to discover this connexion we must, however much we may bristle, take a step beyond it—that is, into metaphysics, although into a region of it different from that of speculative philosophy, namely, the metaphysic of morals.[2] In 427 practical philosophy we are not concerned with accepting reasons for what *happens*, but with accepting laws of what *ought to happen*, even if it never does happen—that is, objective practical laws. And here we have no need to set up an enquiry as to the reasons why anything pleases or displeases; how the pleasure of mere sensation differs from taste, and whether the latter differs from a universal approval by reason;[3] whereon feelings of pleasure and displeasure are based; how from these feelings there arise desires and inclinations; and how from these in turn, with the co-operation of reason, there arise maxims. All this belongs to empirical 63 psychology, which would constitute the second part of the doctrine of nature, if we take this doctrine to be the *philosophy of nature* so far as grounded on *empirical laws*.[1] Here, however, we are discussing objective practical laws, and consequently the relation of a will to itself as determined solely by reason. Everything related to the empirical then falls away of itself; for if *reason entirely by itself* determines conduct (and it is the possibility of this which we now wish to investigate), it must necessarily do so *a priori*.

---

61   *To behold virtue in her proper shape is nothing other than to show morality stripped of all admixture with the sensuous and of all the spurious adornments 62 of reward or self-love. How much she then casts into the shade all else that appears attractive to the inclinations can be readily perceived by every man if he will exert his reason in the slightest—provided he has not entirely ruined it for all abstractions.

[*The Formula of the End in Itself.*]

The will is conceived as a power of determining oneself to action *in accordance with the idea of certain laws*. And such a power can be found only in rational beings. Now what serves the will as a subjective[2] ground of its self-determination is an *end*; and this, if it is given by reason alone, must be equally valid for all rational beings. What, on the other hand, contains merely the ground of the possibility of an action whose effect is an end is called a *means*.[3] The subjective ground of a desire is an *impulsion* (*Triebfeder*); the objective ground of a volition is a *motive* (*Bewegungsgrund*). Hence the difference between subjective ends, which are based on impulsions, and objective ends, which depend 64 on motives valid for every rational being. Practical principles are *formal* if they abstract from all subjective ends; they are *material*, on the other hand, if they are based on such ends and consequently on certain impulsions.[1] Ends that a rational being adopts arbitrarily as *effects* of his action (material ends) are in every case only relative; for it is solely their relation to special characteristics in the subject's power of appetition which gives them their value. Hence this value can provide no universal principles, no principles valid and necessary for all rational beings and also for every volition[2]—that is, no practical laws. Consequently all these relative ends can be the 428 ground only of hypothetical imperatives.

Suppose, however, there were something *whose existence* has *in itself* an absolute value, something which as *an end in itself* could be a ground of determinate laws; then in it, and in it alone, would there be the ground of a possible categorical imperative—that is, of a practical law.

Now I say that man, and in general every rational being, *exists* as an end in himself, *not merely as a means* for arbitrary use by this or that will: he must in all his actions, whether they are directed to himself or to other rational beings, always be viewed *at the same time as an end*. All the objects of inclination have only 65 a conditioned value; for if there were not these inclinations and the needs grounded on them,[1] their object would be valueless. Inclinations themselves, as sources of needs, are so far from having an absolute value to make them desirable for their own sake that it must rather be the universal wish of every rational being to be wholly free from them.[2] Thus the value of all objects that can *be produced* by our action is always conditioned. Beings whose existence depends, not on our will, but on nature, have none the less, if they are non-rational beings, only a relative value as means and are consequently called *things*. Rational beings, on the other hand, are called *persons* because their nature already marks them out as ends in themselves—that is, as something which ought not to be used merely as a means—and consequently imposes to that extent a limit on all arbitrary treatment of them (and is an object of reverence). Persons, therefore, are not merely subjective ends whose existence as an object of our actions has a value *for us*: they are *objective ends*—that is, things whose existence is in itself an end, and indeed an end such that in its place we can put no other end to which they should serve *simply* as means; for unless this is so, nothing at all of *absolute* value would be found anywhere.

66 But if all value were conditioned—that is, contingent—then no supreme principle could be found for reason at all.

If then there is to be a supreme practical principle and—so far as the human will is concerned—a categorical imperative,[1] it must be such that from the idea of something which is necessarily an end for every one because it is an *end in itself* it forms an *objective*

429 principle of the will and consequently can serve as a practical law. The ground of this principle is: *Rational nature exists as an end in itself*. This is the way in which a man necessarily conceives his own existence: it is therefore so far a *subjective* principle of human actions. But it is also the way in which every other rational being conceives his existence on the same rational ground which is valid also for me;* hence it is at the same time an *objective* principle, from which, as a supreme practical ground, it must be possible to derive all laws for the will. The practical imperative will therefore be as follows: *Act in such a way that you always treat humanity,[2] whether in your own person or in the person of any other, never simply[3]*

67 *as a means, but always at the same time as an end*. We will now consider whether this can be carried out in practice.

[*Illustrations*.]

Let us keep to our previous examples.

First, as regards the concept of necessary duty to oneself, the

66   *This proposition I put forward here as a postulate. The grounds for it will be found in the final chapter.[1]

man who contemplates suicide will ask 'Can my action be compatible with the Idea of humanity *as an end in itself?*' If he does away with himself in order to escape from a painful situation, he is making use of a person merely as *a means* to maintain a tolerable state of affairs till the end of his life. But man is not a thing—not something to be used *merely* as a means: he must always in all his actions be regarded as an end in himself. Hence I cannot dispose of man in my person by maiming, spoiling, or killing. (A more precise determination of this principle in order to avoid all misunderstanding—for example, about having limbs amputated to save myself or about exposing my life to danger in order to preserve it, and so on—I must here forego: this question belongs to morals proper.)

Secondly, so far as necessary or strict duty to others is concerned, the man who has a mind to make a false promise to others will see at once that he is intending to make use of another man *merely as a means* to an end he does not share. For the man whom 68 I seek to use for my own purposes by such a promise cannot possibly agree with my way of behaving to him, and so cannot himself share the end of the action. This incompatibility with the 430 principle of duty to others leaps to the eye more obviously when we bring in examples of attempts on the freedom and property of others. For then it is manifest that a violator of the rights of man intends to use the person of others merely as a means without taking into consideration that, as rational beings, they ought always at the same time to be rated as ends—that is, only as beings who must themselves be able to share in the end of the very same action.*

Thirdly, in regard to contingent (meritorious) duty to oneself, it is not enough that an action should refrain from conflicting 69 with humanity in our own person as an end in itself: it must also *harmonize with this end.* Now there are in humanity capacities for greater perfection which form part of nature's purpose for

---

*Let no one think that here the trivial *'quod tibi non vis fieri, etc.'*[1] can serve 68 as a standard or principle. For it is merely derivative from our principle, although subject to various qualifications: it cannot be a universal law[2] since it contains the ground neither of duties to oneself nor of duties of kindness to others (for many a man would readily agree that others should not help him if only he could be dispensed from affording help to them), nor finally of strict duties towards others; for on this basis the criminal would be able to dispute with the judges who punish him, and so on.

humanity in our person.[1] To neglect these can admittedly be compatible with the *maintenance* of humanity as an end in itself, but not with the *promotion* of this end.

Fourthly, as regards meritorious duties to others, the natural end which all men seek is their own happiness. Now humanity could no doubt subsist if everybody contributed nothing to the happiness of others but at the same time refrained from deliberately impairing their happiness. This is, however, merely to agree negatively and not positively with *humanity as an end in itself* unless every one endeavours also, so far as in him lies, to further the ends of others. For the ends of a subject who is an end in himself must, if this conception is to have its *full* effect in me, be also, as far as possible, *my* ends.

[*The Formula of Autonomy.*]

This principle of humanity, and in general of every rational agent, *as an end in itself* (a principle which is the supreme limiting 431] 70 condition of every man's freedom of action) is not borrowed from experience; firstly, because it is universal, applying as it does to all rational beings as such, and no experience is adequate to determine universality; secondly, because in it humanity is conceived, not as an end of man (subjectively)—that is, as an object which, as a matter of fact, happens to be made an end—but as an objective end—one which, be our ends what they may, must, as a law, constitute the supreme limiting condition of all subjective ends and so must spring from pure reason. That is to say, the ground for every enactment of practical law lies *objectively in the rule* and in the form of universality which (according to our first principle) makes the rule capable of being a law (and indeed a law of nature); *subjectively*, however, it lies in the *end*; but (according to our second principle) the subject of all ends is to be found in every rational being as an end in himself. From this there now follows our third practical principle for the will—as the supreme condition of the will's conformity with universal practical reason—namely, the Idea *of the will of every rational being as a will which makes universal law.*

By this principle all maxims are repudiated which cannot accord with the will's own enactment of universal law. The will 71 is therefore not merely subject to the law, but is so subject that it must be considered as also *making the law* for itself and precisely on this account as first of all subject to the law (of which it can regard itself as the author).

[*The exclusion of interest.*]

Imperatives as formulated above—namely, the imperative enjoining conformity of actions to universal law on the analogy of a *natural order* and that enjoining the universal *supremacy* of rational beings in themselves *as ends*—did, by the mere fact that they were represented as categorical, exclude from their sovereign authority every admixture of interest as a motive. They were, however, merely *assumed* to be categorical because we were bound to make this assumption if we wished to explain the concept of duty. That there were practical propositions which commanded categorically could not itself be proved, any more than it can be proved in this chapter generally; but one thing could have been done—namely, to show that in willing for the sake of duty renunciation of all interest,[1] as the specific mark distinguishing a categorical from a hypothetical imperative, was expressed in the very imperative itself by means of some determination inherent in it. This is what is done in the present third formulation of the principle—namely, in the Idea of the will of every rational being as *a will which makes universal law.* 432

Once we conceive a will of this kind, it becomes clear that while a will *which is subject to law* may be bound to this law by some interest, nevertheless a will which is itself a supreme law-giver cannot possibly as such depend on any interest; for a will which is dependent in this way would itself require yet a further law in order to restrict the interest of self-love to the condition that this interest should itself be valid as a universal law.[1] 72

Thus the *principle* that every human will is *a will which by all its maxims enacts universal law**—provided only that it were right in other ways—would be *well suited* to be a categorical imperative in this respect: that precisely because of the Idea of making universal law it is *based on no interest* and consequently can alone among all possible imperatives be *unconditioned*. Or better still—to

---

*I may be excused from bringing forward examples to illustrate this principle, since those which were first used as illustrations of the categorical imperative and its formula can all serve this purpose here. 72

convert the proposition—if there is a categorical imperative (that is, a law for the will of every rational being), it can command us only to act always on the maxim of such a will in us as can
73 at the same time look upon itself as making universal law; for only then is the practical principle and the imperative which we obey unconditioned, since it is wholly impossible for it to be based on any interest.

We need not now wonder, when we look back upon all the previous efforts that have been made to discover the principle of morality, why they have one and all been bound to fail. Their authors saw man as tied to laws by his duty, but it never occurred to them that he is subject only to *laws which are made by himself* and yet are *universal*, and that he is bound only to act in conformity with a will which is his own but has as nature's purpose for it[1] the function of making universal law. For when they thought of man merely as subject to a law (whatever it might be), the law had to
433 carry with it some interest in order to attract or compel, because it did not spring as a law from *his own* will: in order to conform with the law his will had to be necessitated by *something else* to act in a certain way. This absolutely inevitable conclusion meant that all the labour spent in trying to find a supreme principle of duty was lost beyond recall; for what they discovered was never duty, but only the necessity of acting from a certain interest. This interest might be one's own or another's; but on such a view the imperative was bound to be always a conditioned one and
74 could not possibly serve as a moral law. I will therefore call my principle the principle of the *Autonomy* of the will in contrast with all others, which I consequently class under *Heteronomy*.

[*The Formula of the Kingdom of Ends.*]

The concept of every rational being as one who must regard himself as making universal law by all the maxims of his will, and must seek to judge himself and his actions from this point of view, leads to a closely connected and very fruitful concept—namely, that of *a kingdom of ends.*

I understand by a '*kingdom*' a systematic union of different rational beings under common laws. Now since laws determine ends as regards their universal validity, we shall be able—if we abstract from the personal differences between rational beings, and also from all the content of their private ends—to conceive a whole of all ends in systematic conjunction (a whole both of rational beings as ends in themselves and also of the personal ends[1] which each may set before himself); that is, we shall be able to conceive a kingdom of ends which is possible in accordance with the above principles.

For rational beings all stand under the *law* that each of them should treat himself and all others, *never merely as a means*, but 75 always *at the same time as an end in himself*. But by so doing there arises a systematic union of rational beings under common objective laws—that is, a kingdom. Since these laws are directed precisely to the relation of such beings to one another as ends and means, this kingdom can be called a kingdom of ends (which is admittedly only an Ideal).

A rational being belongs to the kingdom of ends as a *member*, when, although he makes its universal laws, he is also himself subject to these laws. He belongs to it as its *head*, when as the maker of laws he is himself subject to the will of no other.[1]

A rational being must always regard himself as making laws 434 in a kingdom of ends which is possible through freedom of the will—whether it be as member or as head. The position of the latter he can maintain, not in virtue of the maxim of his will alone, but only if he is a completely independent being, without needs and with an unlimited power adequate to his will.

Thus morality consists in the relation of all action to the making of laws whereby alone a kingdom of ends is possible. This making of laws must be found in every rational being himself and must 76 be able to spring from his will. The principle of his will is therefore never to perform an action except on a maxim such as can also be a universal law, and consequently such *that the will can regard itself as at the same time making universal law by means of its maxim*. Where maxims are not already by their very nature in harmony with this objective principle of rational beings as makers of universal law, the necessity of acting on this principle is practical necessitation—that is, *duty*. Duty does not apply to the head in a kingdom of ends, but it does apply to every member and to all members in equal measure.

The practical necessity of acting on this principle—that is, duty

—is in no way based on feelings, impulses, and inclinations, but only on the relation of rational beings to one another, a relation in which the will of a rational being must always be regarded as *making universal law*, because otherwise he could not be conceived as *an end in himself*. Reason thus relates every maxim of the will, considered as making universal law, to every other will and also to every action towards oneself: it does so, not because of any further motive or future advantage, but from the Idea of the 77 *dignity* of a rational being who obeys no law other than that which he at the same time enacts himself.

[*The dignity of virtue.*]

In the kingdom of ends everything has either a *price* or a *dignity*. If it has a price, something else can be put in its place as an *equivalent*; if it is exalted above all price and so admits of no equivalent, then it has a dignity.

What is relative to universal human inclinations and needs has a *market price*; what, even without presupposing a need, accords with a certain taste—that is, with satisfaction in the mere purpose-435 less play of our mental powers[1]—has a *fancy price* (*Affektionspreis*); but that which constitutes the sole condition under which anything can be an end in itself has not merely a relative value—that is, a price—but has an intrinsic value—that is, *dignity*.

Now morality is the only condition under which a rational being can be an end in himself; for only through this is it possible to be a law-making member in a kingdom of ends. Therefore morality, and humanity so far as it is capable of morality, is the only thing which has dignity. Skill and diligence in work have a 78 market price; wit, lively imagination, and humour have a fancy price; but fidelity to promises and kindness based on principle (not on instinct) have an intrinsic worth. In default of these, nature and art alike contain nothing to put in their place;[1] for their worth consists, not in the effects which result from them, not in the advantage or profit they produce, but in the attitudes of mind—that is, in the maxims of the will—which are ready in this way to manifest themselves in action even if they are not favoured by success. Such actions too need no recommendation from any subjective disposition or taste in order to meet with immediate

favour and approval; they need no immediate propensity or
feeling for themselves; they exhibit the will which performs them
as an object of immediate reverence; nor is anything other than
reason required to *impose* them upon the will, not to *coax* them
from the will—which last would anyhow be a contradiction in
the case of duties. This assessment reveals as dignity the value of
such a mental attitude and puts it infinitely above all price, with
which it cannot be brought into reckoning or comparison without, as it were, a profanation of its sanctity.

What is it then that entitles a morally good attitude of mind—
or virtue—to make claims so high? It is nothing less than the *share* 79
which it affords to a rational being *in the making of universal law*,
and which therefore fits him to be a member in a possible kingdom
of ends. For this he was already marked out in virtue of his own
proper nature as an end in himself and consequently as a maker
of laws in the kingdom of ends—as free in respect of all laws of
nature, obeying only those laws which he makes himself and in
virtue of which his maxims can have their part in the making
of universal law (to which he at the same time subjects himself). 436
For nothing can have a value other than that determined for it
by the law. But the law-making which determines all value must
for this reason have a dignity—that is, an unconditioned and
incomparable worth—for the appreciation of which, as necessarily
given by a rational being, the word '*reverence*' is the only becoming
expression. *Autonomy* is therefore the ground of the dignity of
human nature and of every rational nature.

[*Review of the Formulae.*]

The aforesaid three ways of representing the principle of morality
are at bottom merely so many formulations of precisely the same
law, one of them by itself containing a combination of the other
two. There is nevertheless a difference between them, which,
however, is subjectively rather than objectively practical: that is
to say, its purpose is to bring an Idea of reason nearer to intuition
(in accordance with a certain analogy) and so nearer to feeling. 80
All maxims have, in short,

1. a *form*, which consists in their universality; and in this
respect the formula of the moral imperative is expressed thus:

'Maxims must be chosen as if they had to hold as universal laws of nature';

2. a *matter*—that is, an end; and in this respect the formula says: 'A rational being, as by his very nature an end and consequently an end in himself, must serve for every maxim as a condition limiting all merely relative and arbitrary ends';

3. a *complete determination*[1] of all maxims by the following formula, namely: 'All maxims as proceeding from our own making of law ought to harmonize with a possible kingdom of ends as a kingdom of nature'.* This progression may be said to take place through the categories of the *unity* of the form of will (its universality); of the *multiplicity* of its matter (its objects—that is, its ends); and of the *totality* or completeness of its system of ends.[2] It is, however, better if in moral *judgement* we proceed always 81 in accordance with the strict method and take as our basis the universal formula of the categorical imperative: '*Act on the maxim* 437 *which can at the same time be made a universal law*'. If, however, we wish also to secure acceptance for the moral law, it is very useful to bring one and the same action under the above-mentioned three concepts and so, as far as we can, to bring the universal formula[1] nearer to intuition.

[Review of the whole argument.]

We can now end at the point from which we started out at the beginning—namely, the concept of an unconditionally good will. The *will* is *absolutely good* if it cannot be evil—that is, if its maxim, when made into a universal law, can never be in conflict with itself. This principle is therefore also its supreme law: 'Act always on that maxim whose universality as a law you can at the same time will'. This is the one principle on which a will can never be in conflict with itself, and such an imperative is categorical. Because the validity of the will as a universal law for possible actions is analogous to the universal interconnexion of existent things in accordance with universal laws—which con-

80   *Teleology views nature as a kingdom of ends; ethics views a possible kingdom of ends as a kingdom of nature. In the first case the kingdom of ends is a theoretical Idea used to explain what exists. In the second case it is a practical Idea used to bring into existence what does not exist but can be made actual by our conduct—and indeed to bring it into existence in conformity with this Idea.

stitutes the formal aspect of nature as such[2]—we can also express
the categorical imperative as follows: '*Act on that maxim which
can at the same time have for its object*[3] *itself as a universal law of
nature*'. In this way we provide the formula for an absolutely good 82
will.

Rational nature separates itself out from all other things by
the fact that it sets itself an end. An end would thus be the matter
of every good will. But in the Idea of a will which is absolutely
good—good without any qualifying condition (namely, that it
should attain this or that end)—there must be complete abstraction
from every end that has to be *produced* (as something which would
make every will only relatively good). Hence the end must here
be conceived, not as an end to be produced, *but as a self-existent*
end. It must therefore be conceived only negatively[1]—that is, as
an end against which we should never act, and consequently as
one which in all our willing we must never rate *merely* as a means,
but always at the same time as an end. Now this end can be
nothing other than the subject of all possible ends himself, because
this subject is also the subject of a will that may be absolutely
good; for such a will cannot without contradiction be subordinated
to any other object. The principle 'So act in relation to every rational
being (both to yourself and to others) that he may at the same time
count in your maxim as an end in himself' is thus at bottom the
same as the principle 'Act on a maxim which at the same time
contains in itself its own universal validity for every rational being'. 438
For to say that in using means to every end I ought to restrict
my maxim by the condition that it should also be universally 83
valid as a law for every subject is just the same as to say this—
that a subject of ends, namely, a rational being himself, must be
made the ground for all maxims of action, never *merely* as a means,
but as a supreme condition restricting the use of every means—
that is, always also as an end.

Now from this it unquestionably follows that every rational
being, as an end in himself, must be able to regard himself as also
the maker of universal law in respect of any law whatever to
which he may be subjected; for it is precisely the fitness of his
maxims to make universal law that marks him out as an end in
himself. It follows equally that this dignity (or prerogative) of his
above all the mere things of nature carries with it the necessity

of always choosing his maxims from the point of view of him-self—and also of every other rational being—as a maker of law (and this is why they are called persons). It is in this way that a world of rational beings (*mundus intelligibilis*) is possible as a kingdom of ends—possible, that is, through the making of their own laws by all persons as its members. Accordingly every rational being must so act as if he were through his maxims always a law-making member in the universal kingdom of ends. The formal principle 84 of such maxims is 'So act as if your maxims had to serve at the same time as a universal law (for all rational beings)'. Thus a kingdom of ends is possible only on the analogy of a kingdom of nature; yet the kingdom of ends is possible only through maxims —that is, self-imposed rules—while nature is possible only through laws concerned with causes whose action is necessitated from without. In spite of this difference, we give to nature as a whole, even although it is regarded as a machine, the name of a 'kingdom of nature' so far as—and for the reason that—it stands in a relation to rational beings as its ends.[1] Now a kingdom of ends would actually come into existence through maxims which the categorical imperative prescribes as a rule for all rational beings, *if these maxims were universally followed*. Yet even if a rational being were himself to follow such a maxim strictly, he cannot count on everybody else being faithful to it on this ground, nor can he be confident that the kingdom of nature and its purposive order will work in harmony with him, as a fitting member, towards a kingdom of ends made possible by himself—or, in other words, that it will 439 favour his expectation of happiness.[2] But in spite of this the law 'Act on the maxims of a member who makes universal laws for a merely possible kingdom of ends' remains in full force, since its command is categorical. And precisely here we encounter the 85 paradox that without any further end or advantage to be attained the mere dignity of humanity, that is, of rational nature in man— and consequently that reverence for a mere Idea—should function as an inflexible precept for the will; and that it is just this freedom from dependence on interested motives which constitutes the sublimity of a maxim and the worthiness of every rational subject to be a law-making member in the kingdom of ends; for other-wise he would have to be regarded as subject only to the law of nature—the law of his own needs. Even if it were thought that both the kingdom of nature and the kingdom of ends were united under one head and that thus the latter kingdom ceased to be a mere Idea and achieved genuine reality, the Idea would indeed gain by this the addition of a strong motive, but never any increase in its intrinsic worth; for, even if this were so, it would still be necessary to conceive the unique and absolute law-giver himself as judging the worth of rational beings solely by the disinterested behaviour they prescribed to themselves in virtue of this Idea alone. The essence of things does not vary with their external relations; and where there is something which, without regard to such relations, constitutes by itself the absolute worth of man, it is by this that man must also be judged by everyone what-soever—even by the Supreme Being. Thus *morality* lies in the relation of actions to the autonomy of the will—that is, to a possible making of universal law by means of its maxims. An 86 action which is compatible with the autonomy of the will is *permitted*; one which does not harmonize with it is *forbidden*. A will whose maxims necessarily accord with the laws of autonomy is a *holy*, or absolutely good, will. The dependence of a will not absolutely good on the principle of autonomy (that is, moral necessitation) is *obligation*. Obligation can thus have no reference to a holy being. The objective necessity to act from obligation is called *duty*.

From what was said a little time ago we can now easily explain how it comes about that, although in the concept of duty we think of subjection to the law, yet we also at the same time attribute to the person who fulfils all his duties a certain sublimity and 440 *dignity*. For it is not in so far as he is *subject* to the law that he has sublimity, but rather in so far as, in regard to this very same law, he is at the same time its *author* and is subordinated to it only on this ground. We have also shown above[1] how neither fear nor inclination, but solely reverence for the law, is the motive which can give an action moral worth. Our own will, provided it were to act only under the condition of being able to make universal 87 law by means of its maxims—this ideal will which can be ours is the proper object of reverence; and the dignity of man consists precisely in his capacity to make universal law, although only on condition of being himself also subject to the law he makes.

AUTONOMY OF THE WILL
as the supreme principle of morality.

Autonomy of the will is the property the will has of being a law to itself (independently of every property belonging to the objects of volition). Hence the principle of autonomy is 'Never to choose except in such a way that in the same volition the maxims of your choice are also present as universal law'. That this practical rule is an imperative—that is, that the will of every rational being is necessarily bound to the rule as a condition—cannot be proved by mere analysis of the concepts contained in it, since it is a synthetic proposition. For proof we should have to go beyond knowledge of objects and pass to a critique of the subject—that is, of pure practical reason—since this synthetic proposition, as commanding apodeictically, must be capable of being known entirely *a priori*. 88 This task does not belong to the present chapter. None the less by mere analysis[1] of the concepts of morality we can quite well show that the above principle of autonomy is the sole principle of ethics. For analysis finds that the principle of morality must be a categorical imperative, and that this in turn commands nothing more nor less than precisely this autonomy.

441 ### HETERONOMY OF THE WILL
as the source of all spurious principles of morality.

If the will seeks the law that is to determine it *anywhere else* than in the fitness of its maxims for its own making of universal law—if therefore in going beyond itself it seeks this law in the character of any of its objects—the result is always *heteronomy*. In that case the will does not give itself the law, but the object does so in virtue of its relation to the will. This relation, whether based on inclination or on rational ideas, can give rise only to hypothetical imperatives: 'I ought to do something *because I will something else*'. As against this, the moral, and therefore categorical, imperative, says: 'I ought to will thus or thus, although I have 89 not willed something else'. For example, the first says: 'I ought not to lie if I want to maintain my reputation'; while the second says: 'I ought not to lie even if so doing were to bring me not the slightest disgrace'. The second imperative must therefore abstract from all objects to this extent—they should be without any *influence*[1] at all on the will so that practical reason (the will) may not merely administer an alien interest but may simply manifest its own sovereign authority as the supreme maker of law. Thus, for example, the reason[2] why I ought to promote the happiness of others is not because the realization of their happiness is of consequence to myself (whether on account of immediate inclination or on account of some satisfaction gained indirectly through reason), but solely because a maxim which excludes this cannot also be present in one and the same volition as a universal law.

CLASSIFICATION

of all possible principles of morality based on the assumption of heteronomy as their fundamental concept.

Here, as everywhere else, human reason in its pure use—so long as it lacks a critique—pursues every possible wrong way before it succeeds in finding the only right one.

All the principles that can be adopted from this point of view are either *empirical* or *rational*. The *first* kind, drawn from the 90 principle of *happiness*, are based either on natural, or on moral, 442 feeling. The *second* kind, drawn from the principle of *perfection*, are based either on the rational concept of perfection as a possible effect of our will or else on the concept of a self-existent perfection (God's will) as a determining cause of our will.

[Empirical principles of heteronomy.]

Empirical principles are always unfitted to serve as a ground for moral laws. The universality with which these laws should hold for all rational beings without exception—the unconditioned practical necessity which they thus impose—falls away if their basis is taken from the *special constitution of human nature* or from the accidental circumstances in which it is placed. The principle of *personal happiness* is, however, the most objectionable, not merely because it is false and because its pretence that well-being always adjusts itself to well-doing is contradicted by experience; nor merely because it contributes nothing whatever towards establishing morality, since making a man happy is quite different

from making him good and making him prudent or astute in seeking his advantage quite different from making him virtuous; but
because it bases morality on sensuous motives which rather undermine it and totally destroy its sublimity, inasmuch as the motives
91 of virtue are put in the same class as those of vice and we are
instructed only to become better at calculation, the specific difference between virtue and vice being completely wiped out. On
the other hand, moral feeling, this alleged special sense* (however
shallow be the appeal to it when men who are unable to *think*
hope to help themselves out by *feeling*, even when the question
is solely one of universal law, and however little feelings, differing
as they naturally do from one another by an infinity of degrees,
can supply a uniform measure of good and evil—let alone that
one man by his feeling can make no valid judgements at all for
others)—moral feeling still remains closer to morality and to its
dignity in this respect: it does virtue the honour of ascribing to
443 her *immediately* the approval and esteem in which she is held, and
does not, as it were, tell her to her face that we are attached to
her, not for her beauty, but only for our own advantage.

[Rational principles of heteronomy.]

Among the *rational* bases of morality—those springing from
92 reason—the ontological concept of *perfection*[1] (however empty,
however indefinite it is, and consequently useless for discovering
in the boundless field of possible reality the maximum reality
appropriate to us; and however much, in trying to distinguish
specifically between the reality here in question and every other,
it shows an inevitable tendency to go round in a circle and is
unable to avoid covertly presupposing the morality it has to explain)
—this concept none the less is better than the theological concept
which derives morality from a divine and supremely perfect will[2];
not merely because we cannot intuit God's perfection and can only
derive it from our own concepts, among which that of morality
is the most eminent; but because, if we do not do this (and to

91   *I class the principle of moral feeling with that of happiness because every
empirical principle promises a contribution to our well-being merely from the
satisfaction afforded by something—whether this satisfaction is given immediately
and without any consideration of advantage or is given in respect of such advantage.
Similarly we must with *Hutcheson*[1] class the principle of sympathy for the happiness
of others along with the principle of moral sense as adopted by him.

do so would be to give a crudely circular explanation), the concept of God's will still remaining to us—one drawn from such characteristics as lust for glory and domination and bound up with frightful ideas of power and vengefulness—would inevitably form the basis for a moral system which would be in direct opposition to morality.

Yet if I had to choose between the concept of moral sense and that of perfection in general[3] (both of which at least do not undermine morality, though they are totally incompetent to support it as its foundation), I should decide for the latter; for this, since it 93 at least withdraws the settlement of this question from sensibility and brings it before the court of pure reason, even although it there gets no decision, does still preserve unfalsified for more precise determination the indeterminate Idea (of a will good in itself).

[The failure of heteronomy.]

For the rest I believe I may be excused from a lengthy refutation of all these systems. This is so easy and is presumably so well understood even by those whose office requires them to declare themselves for one or other of these theories (since their audience will not lightly put up with a suspension of judgement) that to spend time on it would be merely superfluous labour. But what is of more interest to us here is to know that these principles never lay down anything but heteronomy as the first basis of morality and must in consequence necessarily fail in their object.

Wherever an object of the will has to be put down as the basis 444 for prescribing a rule to determine the will, there the rule is heteronomy; the imperative is conditioned, as follows: '*If*, or *because*, you will this object, you ought to act thus or thus'; consequently it can never give a moral—that is, a categorical—command. However the object determines the will—whether by means of inclination, as in the principle of personal happiness, or by 94 means of reason directed to objects of our possible volitions generally, as in the principle of perfection—the will never determines itself *immediately* by the thought of an action, but only by the impulsion which the anticipated effect of the action exercises on the will: '*I ought to do something because I will something else*'.

And the basis for this must be yet a further law in me as a subject, whereby I necessarily will this 'something else'—which law in turn requires an imperative to impose limits on this maxim.[1] The impulsion supposed to be exercised on the will of the subject, in accordance with his natural constitution, by the idea of a result to be attained by his own powers belongs to the nature of the subject—whether to his sensibility (his inclinations and taste) or to his understanding and reason, whose operation on an object is accompanied by satisfaction in virtue of the special equipment of their nature—and consequently, speaking strictly, it is nature which would make the law. This law, as a law of nature, not only must be known and proved by experience and therefore is in itself contingent and consequently unfitted to serve as an apodeictic rule of action such as a moral rule must be, but it is *always merely heteronomy of the will*: the will does not give itself the law, but an 95 alien impulsion does so through the medium of the subject's own nature as tuned for its reception.

[*The position of the argument.*]

An absolutely good will, whose principle must be a categorical imperative, will therefore, being undetermined in respect of all objects, contain only the *form* of *willing*, and that as autonomy. In other words, the fitness of the maxim of every good will to make itself a universal law is itself the sole law which the will of every rational being spontaneously imposes on itself without basing it on any impulsion or interest.

How such a synthetic a priori *proposition is possible* and why it is necessary—this is a problem whose solution lies no longer within 445 the bounds of a metaphysic of morals; nor have we here asserted the truth of this proposition, much less pretended to have a proof of it in our power. We have merely shown by developing the concept of morality generally in vogue that autonomy of the will is unavoidably bound up with it or rather is its very basis. Any one therefore who takes morality to be something, and not merely a chimerical Idea without truth, must at the same time admit the 96 principle we have put forward. This chapter, consequently, like the first, has been merely analytic. In order to prove that morality is no mere phantom of the brain—a conclusion which follows if the categorical imperative, and with it the autonomy of the will, is true and is absolutely necessary as an *a priori* principle—we require a *possible synthetic use of pure practical reason*.[1] On such a use we cannot venture without prefacing it by a *critique* of this power of reason itself—a critique whose main features, so far as is sufficient for our purpose, we must outline in our final chapter.

CHAPTER III

PASSAGE FROM A METAPHYSIC
OF MORALS TO A
CRITIQUE OF PURE PRACTICAL REASON

THE CONCEPT OF FREEDOM
IS THE KEY TO EXPLAIN AUTONOMY OF THE WILL

WILL is a kind of causality belonging to living beings so far as they are rational. *Freedom* would then be the property this causality has of being able to work independently of *determination* by alien causes; just as *natural necessity* is a property characterizing the causality of all non-rational beings—the property of being determined to activity by the influence of alien causes.

The above definition of freedom is *negative* and consequently unfruitful as a way of grasping its essence; but there springs from it a *positive* concept, which, as positive, is richer and more fruitful. The concept of causality carries with it that of *laws (Gesetze)* in accordance with which, because of something we call a cause, 98 something else—namely, its effect—must be posited *(gesetzt)*. Hence freedom of will, although it is not the property of conforming to laws of nature, is not for this reason lawless: it must rather be a causality conforming to immutable laws, though of a special kind; for otherwise a free will would be self-contradictory. Natural necessity, as we have seen, is a heteronomy of efficient causes; for every effect is possible only in conformity with the law that something else determines the efficient cause to causal 447 action. What else then can freedom of will be but autonomy— that is, the property which will has of being a law to itself? The proposition 'Will is in all its actions a law to itself' expresses, however, only the principle of acting on no maxim other than one which can have for its object[1] itself as at the same time a universal law. This is precisely the formula of the categorical imperative and the principle of morality. Thus a free will and a will under moral laws are one and the same.[2]

114

Consequently if freedom of the will is presupposed, morality, together with its principle, follows by mere analysis of the concept of freedom. Nevertheless the principle of morality is still a synthetic proposition, namely: 'An absolutely good will is one whose maxim can always have as its content itself considered as a universal law'; for we cannot discover this characteristic of its maxim by analysing 99 the concept of an absolutely good will. Such synthetic propositions are possible only because two cognitions[1] are bound to one another by their connexion with a third term in which both of them are to be found. The *positive* concept of freedom furnishes this third term, which cannot, as in the case of physical causes, be the nature of the sensible world (in the concept of which there come together the concepts of something as cause and of *something else* as effect in their relation to one another). What this third term is to which freedom directs us and of which we have an Idea *a priori*, we are not yet in a position to show here straight away,[2] nor can we as yet make intelligible the deduction of the concept of freedom from pure practical reason and so the possibility of a categorical imperative: we require some further preparation.

FREEDOM MUST BE PRESUPPOSED AS A PROPERTY OF THE WILL OF ALL RATIONAL BEINGS

It is not enough to ascribe freedom to our will, on whatever ground, unless we have sufficient reason for attributing the same freedom to all rational beings as well. For since morality is a law 100 for us only as *rational beings*, it must be equally valid for all rational beings; and since it must be derived solely from the property of freedom, we have got to prove that freedom too is a property of the will of all rational beings. It is not enough to demonstrate freedom from certain alleged experiences of human nature (though to do this is in any case absolutely impossible and freedom can be 448 demonstrated only *a priori*)[1]: we must prove that it belongs universally to the activity of rational beings endowed with a will. Now I assert that every being who cannot act except *under the Idea of freedom* is by this alone—from a practical point of view— really free; that is to say, for him all the laws inseparably bound up with freedom are valid just as much as if his will could be pronounced free in itself on grounds valid for theoretical

philosophy.* And I maintain that to every rational being possessed
101 of a will we must also lend the Idea of freedom as the only one
under which he can act. For in such a being we conceive a reason
which is practical—that is, which exercises causality in regard to
its objects. But we cannot possibly conceive of a reason as being
consciously directed from outside in regard to its judgements[1];
for in that case the subject would attribute the determination of his
power of judgement, not to his reason, but to an impulsion.
Reason must look upon itself as the author of its own principles
independently of alien influences. Therefore as practical reason,[2]
or as the will of a rational being, it must be regarded by itself
as free; that is, the will of a rational being can be a will of his
own only under the Idea of freedom, and such a will must therefore—from a practical point of view—be attributed to all rational
beings.

The Interest Attached to the Ideas of Morality
[Moral interest and the vicious circle.]

We have at last traced the determinate concept of morality
back to the Idea of freedom, but we have been quite unable to
demonstrate freedom as something actual in ourselves and in human
449 nature: we saw merely that we must presuppose it if we wish to
102 conceive a being as rational and as endowed with consciousness
of his causality in regard to actions—that is, as endowed with a
will. Thus we find that on precisely the same ground we must
attribute to every being endowed with reason and a will this
property of determining himself to action under the Idea of his
own freedom.[1]

From the presupposition of this Idea[2] there springs, as we
further saw, consciousness of a law of action, the law that subjective principles of action—that is, maxims—must always be
adopted in such a way that they can also hold as principles
objectively—that is, universally—and can therefore serve for our
own enactment of universal law. But why should I subject myself

100   *This method takes it as sufficient for our purpose if freedom is presupposed
merely as an Idea by all rational beings in their actions; and I adopt it in order to
avoid the obligation of having to prove freedom from a theoretical point of view
as well. For even if this latter problem is left unsettled, the same laws as would bind
a being who was really free are equally valid for a being who cannot act except
under the Idea of his own freedom. In this way we can relieve ourselves of the
burden which weighs upon theory.[1]

to this principle simply as a rational being and in so doing also subject to it every other being endowed with reason? I am willing to admit that no interest *impels* me to do so since this would not produce a categorical imperative; but all the same I must necessarily *take* an interest in it and understand how this happens; for this 'I ought' is properly an 'I will' which holds necessarily for every rational being—provided that reason in him is practical without any hindrance. For beings who, like us, are affected also by sensibility—that is, by motives of a different kind—and who do not always act as reason by itself would act, this necessity is expressed 103 as an 'I ought,' and the subjective necessity is distinct from the objective one.[1]

It looks as if, in our Idea of freedom, we have in fact merely taken the moral law for granted—that is, the very principle of the autonomy of the will—and have been unable to give an independent proof of its reality and objective necessity. In that case we should still have made a quite considerable gain inasmuch as we should at least have formulated the genuine principle more precisely than has been done before. As regards its validity, however, and the practical necessity of subjecting ourselves to it we should have got no further. Why must the validity of our maxim as a universal law be a condition limiting our action? On what do we base the worth we attach to this way of acting—a worth supposed to be so great that there cannot be any interest which is higher? And how does it come about that in this alone man believes himself to feel his own personal worth, in comparison with which that 450 of a pleasurable or painful state is to count as nothing? To these questions we should have been unable to give any sufficient answer.

We do indeed find ourselves able to take an interest in a personal characteristic which carries with it no interest in mere states,[1] but 104 only makes us fit to have a share in such states in the event of their being distributed by reason. That is to say, the mere fact of deserving happiness can by itself interest us even without the motive of getting a share in this happiness. Such a judgement, however, is in fact merely the result of the importance we have already assumed to belong to moral laws (when we detach ourselves from every empirical interest by our Idea of freedom). But on this basis we can as yet have no insight into the principle that we ought to detach ourselves from such interest—that is, that we ought to regard ourselves as free in our actions and yet to hold ourselves bound by certain laws in order to find solely in our own person a worth which can compensate us for the loss of everything that makes our state valuable. We do not see how this is possible nor consequently *how the moral law can be binding.*

In this, we must frankly admit, there is shown a kind of circle, from which, as it seems, there is no way of escape. In the order of efficient causes we take ourselves to be free so that we may conceive ourselves to be under moral laws in the order of ends; and we then proceed to think of ourselves as subject to moral laws on the ground that we have described our will as free. Freedom and the will's enactment of its own laws are indeed both autonomy 105 —and therefore are reciprocal concepts[1]—but precisely for this reason one of them cannot be used to explain the other or to furnish its ground. It can at most be used for logical purposes in order to bring seemingly different ideas of the same object under a single concept (just as different fractions of equal value can be reduced to their simplest expression).

[*The two standpoints.*]

One shift, however, still remains open to us. We can enquire whether we do not take one standpoint when by means of freedom we conceive ourselves as causes acting *a priori*, and another standpoint when we contemplate ourselves with reference to our actions as effects which we see before our eyes.

One observation is possible without any need for subtle reflexion and, we may assume, can be made by the most ordinary intelligence—no doubt in its own fashion through some obscure 451 discrimination of the power of judgement known to it as 'feeling.' The observation is this—that all ideas coming to us apart from our own volition (as do those of the senses) enable us to know objects only as they affect ourselves: what they may be in themselves remains unknown. Consequently, ideas of this kind, even 106 with the greatest effort of attention and clarification brought to bear by understanding, serve only for knowledge of *appearances,* never of *things in themselves.* Once this distinction is made (it may be merely by noting the difference between ideas given to us from without, we ourselves being passive, and those which we produce entirely from ourselves, and so manifest our own activity), it follows of itself that behind appearances we must admit and assume something else which is not appearance—namely, things in themselves —although, since we can never be acquainted with these, but only with the way in which they affect us, we must resign ourselves to the fact that we can never get any nearer to them and can never know what they are in themselves. This must yield us a distinction, however rough, between the *sensible world* and the *intelligible world*, the first of which can vary a great deal according to differences of sensibility in sundry observers, while the second, which is its ground, always remains the same. Even as regards himself—so far as man is acquainted with himself by inner sensation[1]—he cannot claim to know what he is in himself. For since he does not, so to say, make himself, and since he acquires his concept of self not *a priori* but empirically, it is natural that even about himself he should get information through sense—that is, through inner sense—and consequently only through the mere appearance of his own nature and through the way in which his 107 consciousness is affected. Yet beyond this character of himself as a subject[1] made up, as it is, of mere appearances he must suppose there to be something else which is its ground—namely, his Ego as this may be constituted in itself; and thus as regards mere perception and the capacity for receiving sensations[2] he must count himself as belonging to the *sensible world*, but as regards whatever there may be in him of pure activity (whatever comes into consciousness, not through affection of the senses, but immediately)[3] he must count himself as belonging to the *intellectual world*, of which, however, he knows nothing further.

A conclusion of this kind must be reached by a thinking man about everything that may be presented to him. It is presumably 452 to be found even in the most ordinary intelligence, which, as is well known, is always very much disposed to look behind the objects of the senses for something further that is invisible and is spontaneously active; but it goes on to spoil this by immediately sensifying this invisible something in its turn—that is to say, it wants to make it an object of intuition, and so by this procedure it does not become in any degree wiser.

Now man actually finds in himself a power which distinguishes him from all other things—and even from himself so far as he is 108 affected by objects. This power is *reason*.[1] As pure spontaneity reason is elevated even above *understanding* in the following respect. Understanding—although it too is spontaneous activity and is not, like sense, confined to ideas which arise only when we are affected by things (and therefore are passive)—understanding cannot produce by its own activity any concepts other than those whose sole service is *to bring sensuous ideas under rules* and so to unite them in one consciousness: without this employment of sensibility it would think nothing at all. Reason, on the other hand—in what are called 'Ideas'—shows a spontaneity so pure that it goes far beyond anything sensibility can offer: it manifests its highest function in distinguishing the sensible and intelligible worlds from one another and so in marking out limits for understanding itself.[2]

Because of this a rational being must regard himself *qua intelligence* (and accordingly not on the side of his lower faculties) as belonging to the intelligible world, not to the sensible one. He has therefore two points of view from which he can regard himself and from which he can know laws governing the employment of his powers and consequently governing all his actions. He can consider himself *first*—so far as he belongs to the sensible 109 world—to be under laws of nature (heteronomy); and *secondly*—so far as he belongs to the intelligible world—to be under laws which, being independent of nature, are not empirical but have their ground in reason alone.

As a rational being, and consequently as belonging to the intelligible world, man can never conceive the causality of his own will except under the Idea of freedom; for to be independent of determination by causes in the sensible world (and this is what reason must always attribute to itself) is to be free. To the Idea of freedom there is inseparably attached the concept of *autonomy*, and to this in turn the universal principle of morality—a principle 453 which in Idea[1] forms the ground for all the actions of *rational* beings, just as the law of nature does for all appearances.

The suspicion which we raised above is now removed—namely, that there might be a hidden circle in our inference from freedom to autonomy and from autonomy to the moral law; that in effect we had perhaps assumed the Idea of freedom only because of the moral law in order subsequently to infer the moral law in its turn from freedom; and that consequently we had been able to assign no ground at all for the moral law, but had merely assumed it by begging a principle which well-meaning souls will gladly concede us, but which we could never put forward as a demonstrable proposi- 110 tion. We see now that when we think of ourselves as free, we transfer ourselves into the intelligible world as members and recognize the autonomy of the will together with its consequence— morality; whereas when we think of ourselves as under obligation, we look upon ourselves as belonging to the sensible world and yet to the intelligible world at the same time.

How is a Categorical Imperative Possible?

A rational being counts himself, *qua* intelligence, as belonging to the intelligible world, and solely *qua* efficient cause belonging to the intelligible world does he give to his causality the name of '*will*'. On the other side, however, he is conscious of himself as also a part of the sensible world, where his actions are encountered as mere appearances of this causality. Yet the possibility of these actions cannot be made intelligible by means of such causality, since with this we have no direct acquaintance; and instead these actions, as belonging to the sensible world, have to be understood as determined by other appearances—namely, by desires and inclinations. Hence, if I were solely a member of the intelligible world, all my actions would be in perfect conformity with the principle of the autonomy of a pure will; if I were solely a part of the sensible world, they would have to be taken as in complete conformity with the law of nature governing desires and inclina-tions—that is, with the heteronomy of nature. (In the first case 111 they would be grounded on the supreme principle of morality; in the second case on that of happiness.) *But the intelligible world contains the ground of the sensible world and therefore also of its laws;* and so in respect of my will, for which (as belonging entirely to the intelligible world) it gives laws immediately,[1] it must also be conceived as containing such a ground.[2] Hence, in spite of regard-ing myself from one point of view as a being that belongs to the sensible world, I shall have to recognize that, *qua* intelligence, I 454 am subject to the law of the intelligible world—that is, to the reason which contains this law in the Idea of freedom, and so to the autonomy of the will—and therefore I must look on the laws of the intelligible world as imperatives for me and on the actions which conform to this principle as duties.

And in this way categorical imperatives are possible because the Idea of freedom makes me a member of an intelligible world. This being so, if I were solely a member of the intelligible world, all my actions *would* invariably accord with the autonomy of the will; but because I intuit myself at the same time as a member of the sensible world, they *ought* so to accord. This *categorical* 'ought' presents us with a synthetic *a priori* proposition, since to my will as affected by sensuous desires there is added the Idea of the same will,[3] viewed, however, as a pure will belonging to the intelligible 112 world and active on its own account—a will which contains the supreme condition of the former will, so far as reason is concerned. This is roughly like the way in which concepts of the understanding, which by themselves signify nothing but the form of law in general, are added to intuitions of the sensible world and so make synthetic *a priori* propositions possible on which all our knowledge of nature is based.

The practical use of ordinary human reason confirms the rightness of this deduction. There is no one, not even the most hardened scoundrel—provided only he is accustomed to use reason in other ways—who, when presented with examples of honesty in purpose, of faithfulness to good maxims, of sympathy, and of kindness towards all (even when these are bound up with great sacrifices of advantage and comfort), does not wish that he too might be a man of like spirit. He is unable to realize such an aim in his own person—though only on account of his desires and impulses; but yet at the same time he wishes to be free from these inclinations, which are a burden to himself. By such a wish he shows that having a will free from sensuous impulses he transfers himself in thought into an order of things quite different from that of his desires in the field of sensibility; for from the fulfilment of this wish he can expect no gratification of his sensuous desires and consequently no state which would satisfy any of his actual or 113 even conceivable inclinations (since by such an expectation the very Idea which elicited the wish would be deprived of its superiority); all he can expect is a greater inner worth of his own 455 person. This better person he believes himself to be when he transfers himself to the standpoint of a member of the intelligible world. He is involuntarily constrained to do so by the Idea of freedom—that is, of not being dependent on *determination* by causes in the sensible world; and from this standpoint he is conscious of possessing a good will which, on his own admission, constitutes the law for the bad will belonging to him as a member of the sensible world—a law of whose authority he is aware even in transgressing it. The moral 'I ought' is thus an 'I will' for man as a member of the intelligible world; and it is conceived by him as an 'I ought' only in so far as he considers himself at the same time to be a member of the sensible world.

THE EXTREME LIMIT OF PRACTICAL PHILOSOPHY
[*The antinomy of freedom and necessity.*]

All men think of themselves as having a free will. From this arise all judgements that actions are such as *ought to have been done*, although they *have not been done*. This freedom is no concept of experience, nor can it be such, since it continues to hold although experience shows the opposite of those requirements which are regarded as necessary[1] under the presupposition of freedom. On 114 the other hand, it is just as necessary that everything which takes place should be infallibly determined in accordance with the laws of nature; and this necessity of nature is likewise no concept of experience, precisely because it carries with it the concept of necessity and so of *a priori* knowledge. The concept of nature is, however, confirmed by experience and must inevitably be presupposed if experience—that is, coherent knowledge of sensible objects in accordance with universal laws—is to be possible. Hence, while freedom is only an *Idea* of reason whose objective reality is in itself questionable, nature is a *concept of the understanding*, which proves, and must necessarily prove, its reality in examples from experience.

From this there arises a dialectic[2] of reason, since the freedom attributed to the will seems incompatible with the necessity of nature; and although at this parting of the ways reason finds the road of natural necessity much more beaten and serviceable than that of freedom for *purposes of speculation*, yet for *purposes of action* the footpath of freedom is the only one on which we can make use of reason in our conduct. Hence to argue freedom away is 456 as impossible for the most abstruse philosophy as it is for the most 115 ordinary human reason. Reason must therefore suppose that no genuine contradiction is to be found between the freedom and the natural necessity ascribed to the very same human actions; for it can abandon the concept of nature as little as it can abandon that of freedom.

All the same we must at least get rid of this seeming contradiction in a convincing fashion—although we shall never be able to comprehend how freedom is possible. For if the thought of freedom is self-contradictory or incompatible with nature—a concept which is equally necessary—freedom would have to be completely abandoned in favour of natural necessity.

[*The two standpoints.*]

From this contradiction it would be impossible to escape if the subject who believes himself free were to conceive himself *in the same sense*, or *in precisely the same relationship*, when he calls himself free as when he holds himself subject to the law of nature in respect of the same action. Hence speculative philosophy has the unavoidable task of showing at least this—that its illusion about the contradiction rests on our conceiving man in one sense and relationship when we call him free and in another when we consider 116 him, as a part of nature, to be subject to nature's laws; and that both characteristics not merely *can* get on perfectly well together, but must be conceived as *necessarily combined* in the same subject; for otherwise we could not explain why we should trouble reason with an Idea which—even if it can *without contradiction* be combined with a different and adequately verified concept—does yet involve us in a business which puts reason to sore straits in its theoretical use. This duty is incumbent on speculative philosophy solely in order that it may clear a path for practical philosophy. Thus it is not left to the discretion of philosophers whether they will remove the seeming contradiction or leave it untouched; for in the latter case the theory on this topic becomes *bonum vacans*,[1] of which the fatalist can justifiably take possession and can chase all morality out of its supposed property, which it has no title to hold.

Nevertheless at this point we cannot yet say that the boundary of practical philosophy begins. For practical philosophy has no part in the settlement of this controversy: it merely requires specula- 457 tive reason to bring to an end the dissension in which it is entangled on theoretical questions so that practical reason may have peace and security from external attacks capable of bringing into dispute the territory it seeks to cultivate.

The lawful title to freedom of will claimed even by ordinary 117 human reason is grounded on a consciousness—and an accepted presupposition—that reason is independent of purely subjective determination by causes which collectively make up all that belongs to sensation and comes under the general name of sensibility. In thus regarding himself as intelligence man puts himself into another order of things, and into relation with determining causes of quite another sort, when he conceives himself as intelligence endowed with a will and consequently with causality, than he does when he perceives himself as a phenomenon in the sensible world (which he actually is as well) and subjects his causality to external determination in accordance with laws of nature. He then becomes aware at once that both of these can, and indeed must, take place at the same time; for there is not the slightest contradiction in holding that a *thing as an appearance* (as belonging to the sensible world) is subject to certain laws of which it is independent *as a thing* or being *in itself*. That he must represent and conceive himself in this double way rests, as regards the first side, on consciousness of himself as an object affected through the senses; as concerns the second side, on consciousness of himself as intelligence—that is, as independent of sensuous impressions in his use of reason (and so as belonging to the intelligible world).

Hence it comes about that man claims for himself a will which 118 does not impute to itself anything appertaining merely to his desires and inclinations; and, on the other hand, that he conceives as possible through its agency, and indeed as necessary, actions which can be done only by disregarding all desires and incitements of sense. The causality of such actions lies in man as intelligence and in the laws of such effects and actions as accord with the principles of an intelligible world. Of that world he knows[1] no more than this—that in it reason alone, and indeed pure reason independent of sensibility, is the source of law; and also that since he is there his proper self only as intelligence (while as a human being he is merely an appearance of himself), these laws apply to him immediately[2] and categorically. It follows that incitements from desires and impulses (and therefore from the whole sensible world of nature) cannot impair the laws which govern his will 458 as intelligence. Indeed he does not answer for the former nor impute them to his proper self—that is, to his will; but he does impute to himself the indulgence which he would show them if he admitted their influence on his maxims to the detriment of the rational laws governing his will.

[There is no knowledge of the intelligible world.]

By *thinking* itself into the intelligible world practical reason does not overstep its limits in the least: it would do so only if it sought to *intuit or feel itself* into that world. The thought in question 119 is a merely negative one with respect to the sensible world: it gives reason no laws for determining the will and is positive only in this one point, that it combines freedom as a negative characteristic with a (positive) power as well—and indeed with a causality of reason called by us 'a will'—a power so to act that the principle of our actions may accord with the essential character of a rational cause, that is, with the condition that the maxim of these actions should have the validity of a universal law. If practical reason were also to import an *object of the will*—that is, a motive of action—from the intelligible world, it would overstep its limits and pretend to an acquaintance with something of which it has no knowledge. The concept of the intelligible world is thus only *a point of view*[1] which reason finds itself constrained to adopt outside appearances *in order to conceive itself as practical*. To conceive itself thus would not be possible if the influences of sensibility were able to determine man; but it is none the less necessary so far as we are not to deny him consciousness of himself as intelligence and consequently as a rational cause which is active by means of reason—that is, which is free in its operation. This thought admittedly carries with it the Idea of an order and a legislation different from that of the mechanism of nature appropriate to the world of sense. It makes necessary the concept of an intelligible world (that is, of the totality of rational beings as things in themselves); but it makes not the 120 slightest pretension to do more than conceive such a world with respect to its *formal* condition—to conceive it, that is, as conforming to the condition that the maxim of the will should have the universality of a law, and so as conforming to the autonomy of the will, which alone is compatible with freedom. In contrast with this all laws determined by reference to an object give us heteronomy, which can be found only in laws of nature and can apply only to the world of sense.

[There is no explanation of freedom.]

Reason would overstep all its limits if it took upon itself to *explain how* pure reason can be practical. This would be identical with the task of explaining *how freedom is possible.*

459

We are unable to explain anything unless we can bring it under laws which can have an object given in some possible experience. Freedom, however, is a mere Idea: its objective validity can in no way be exhibited by reference to laws of nature and consequently cannot be exhibited in any possible experience. Thus the Idea of freedom can never admit of full comprehension, or indeed of insight,[1] since it can never by any analogy have an example falling under it. It holds only as a necessary presupposition of reason in a being who believes himself to be conscious of a will—that is, of a power distinct from mere appetition (a power, namely, of determining himself to act as intelligence and consequently to act in accordance with laws of reason independently of natural instincts). 121 But where determination by laws of nature comes to an end, all *explanation* comes to an end as well. Nothing is left but *defence*— that is, to repel the objections of those who profess to have seen more deeply into the essence of things and on this ground audaciously declare freedom to be impossible. We can only show them that their pretended discovery of a contradiction in it consists in nothing but this: in order to make the law of nature apply to human actions they have necessarily had to consider man as an appearance; and now that they are asked to conceive him, *qua* intelligence, as a thing in himself as well, they continue to look upon him as an appearance in this respect also. In that case, admittedly, to exempt man's causality (that is, his will) from all the natural laws of the sensible world would, in one and the same subject, give rise to a contradiction. The contradiction would fall away if they were willing to reflect and to admit, as is reasonable, that things in themselves (although hidden) must lie behind appearances as their ground, and that we cannot require the laws of their operations to be identical with those that govern their appearances.

[*There is no explanation of moral interest.*]

The subjective impossibility of *explaining* freedom of will is 122 the same as the impossibility of finding out and making compre-460 hensible what *interest***** man can take in moral laws; and yet he does in fact take such an interest. The basis of this in ourselves we call 'moral feeling'. Some people have mistakenly given out this feeling to be the gauge of our moral judgements: it should be regarded rather as the *subjective* effect exercised on our will by the law and having its objective ground in reason alone.

If we are to will actions for which reason by itself prescribes an 'ought' to a rational, yet sensuously affected, being, it is admittedly necessary that reason should have a power of *infusing* a *feeling of pleasure* or satisfaction in the fulfilment of duty,[1] and consequently that it should possess a kind of causality by which 123 it can determine sensibility in accordance with rational principles. It is, however, wholly impossible to comprehend—that is, to make intelligible *a priori*—how a mere thought containing nothing sensible in itself can bring about a sensation of pleasure or dis-pleasure; for there is here a special kind of causality, and—as with all causality—we are totally unable to determine its character *a priori*: on this we must consult experience alone. The latter can-not provide us with a relation of cause and effect except between two objects of experience—whereas here pure reason by means of mere Ideas (which furnish absolutely no objects for experience) has to be the cause of an effect admittedly found in experience. Hence for us men it is wholly impossible to explain how and why the *universality of a maxim as a law*—and therefore morality—should interest us. This much only is certain: the law is not valid for us *because it interests us* (for this is heteronomy and makes practical

---

122 *An interest is that in virtue of which reason becomes practical—that is, becomes a cause determining the will. Hence only of a rational being do we say that he takes an interest in something: non-rational creatures merely feel sensuous impulses. Reason takes an immediate interest in an action only when the universal validity of the maxim of the action is a ground sufficient to determine the will. Such an interest alone is pure. When reason is able to determine the will only by means of some further object of desire or under the presupposition of some special feeling in the subject, then it takes only a mediate interest in the action; and since reason entirely by itself without the aid of experience can discover neither objects for the will nor a special feeling underlying the will, the latter interest would be merely empirical, and not a pure rational interest. The logical interest of reason (interest in promoting its own insight) is never immediate, but presupposes purposes for which reason can be employed.

reason depend on sensibility—that is to say, on an underlying 461 feeling—in which case practical reason could never give us moral law); the law interests us because it is valid for us as men in virtue of having sprung from our will as intelligence and so from our proper self; *but what belongs to mere appearance is necessarily subordinated by reason to the character of the thing in itself.*

[General review of the argument.]

Thus the question 'How is a categorical imperative possible?' 124 can be answered so far as we can supply the sole presupposition under which it is possible—namely, the Idea of freedom—and also so far as we can have insight into the necessity of this presupposition. This is sufficient for the *practical use* of reason—that is, for conviction of the *validity of this imperative*, and so too of the moral law. But how this presupposition itself is possible is never open to the insight of any human reason. Yet, on the presupposition that the will of an intelligence is free, there follows necessarily its *autonomy* as the formal condition under which alone it can be determined. It is not only perfectly *possible* (as speculative philosophy can show) to presuppose such freedom of the will (without contradicting the principle that natural necessity governs the connexion of appearances in the sensible world); it is also *necessary*, without any further condition, for a rational being conscious of exercising causality by means of reason and so of having a will (which is distinct from desires) to make such freedom in practice—that is, in Idea—underlie all his voluntary actions as their condition.[1] But *how* pure reason can be practical in itself without further motives drawn from some other source; that is, how the bare *principle of the universal validity of all its maxims as laws* (which would admittedly 125 be the form of a pure practical reason) can by itself—without any matter (or object) of the will in which we could take some antecedent interest—supply a motive and create an interest which could be called purely *moral*; or, in other words, *how pure reason can be practical*—all human reason is totally incapable of explaining this, and all the effort and labour to seek such an explanation is wasted.

It is precisely the same as if I sought to fathom how freedom itself is possible as the causality of a will. There I abandon a philosophical basis[1] of explanation, and I have no other. I could, 462 no doubt, proceed to flutter about in the intelligible world, which still remains left to me—the world of intelligences; but although I have an *Idea* of it, which has its own good grounds, yet I have not the slightest *acquaintance* with such a world, nor can I ever attain such acquaintance by all the efforts of my natural power of reason. My Idea signifies only a 'something' that remains over when I have excluded from the grounds determining my will everything that belongs to the world of sense: its sole purpose is to restrict the principle that all motives come from the field of sensibility, by setting bounds to this field and by showing that it does not comprise all in all within itself, but that there is still more

126 beyond it; yet with this 'more' I have no further acquaintance. Of the pure reason which conceives this Ideal, after I have set aside all matter—that is, all knowledge of objects—there remains nothing over for me except its form—namely, the practical law that maxims should be universally valid—and the corresponding conception of reason, in its relation to a purely intelligible world, as a possible efficient cause, that is, a cause determining the will. Here all sensuous motives must entirely fail; this Idea of an intelligible world would itself have to be the motive or to be that wherein reason originally took an interest. To make this comprehensible is, however, precisely the problem that we are unable to solve.

[*The extreme limit of moral enquiry.*]

Here then is the extreme limit of all moral enquiry. To determine this limit is, however, of great importance in this respect: by so doing reason may be kept, on the one hand, from searching around in the sensible world—greatly to the detriment of morality —for the supreme motive and for some interest, comprehensible indeed, but empirical; and it may be kept, on the other hand, from flapping its wings impotently, without leaving the spot, in a space that for it is empty—the space of transcendent concepts known as 'the intelligible world'—and so from getting lost among mere phantoms of the brain. For the rest, the Idea of a purely intelligible world, as a whole of all intelligences to which we ourselves belong as rational beings (although from another point of view we are members of the sensible world as well), remains always a serviceable and permitted Idea for the purposes of a rational belief, though all

knowledge ends at its boundary: it serves to produce in us a lively **127**
interest in the moral law by means of the splendid ideal of a universal kingdom of *ends in themselves* (rational beings), to which
we can belong as members only if we are scrupulous to live in **463**
accordance with maxims of freedom as if they were laws of nature.

CONCLUDING NOTE

The speculative use of reason *in regard to nature* leads to the
absolute necessity of some supreme cause of the *world*; the practical
use of reason *with respect to freedom* leads also to absolute necessity—
but only to the absolute necessity *of the laws of action* for a rational
being as such. Now it is an essential *principle* for every use of reason
to push its knowledge to the point where we are conscious of its
necessity (for without necessity it would not be knowledge characteristic of reason). It is an equally essential *limitation* of the same
reason that it cannot have insight into the *necessity* either of what
is or what happens, or of what ought to happen, except on the
basis of a *condition* under which it is or happens or ought to happen.
In this way, however, the satisfaction of reason is merely postponed **128**
again and again by continual enquiry after a condition. Hence
reason unrestingly seeks the unconditionally necessary and sees
itself compelled to assume this without any means of making it
comprehensible—happy enough if only it can find a concept
compatible with this presupposition. Thus it is no discredit to our
deduction of the supreme principle of morality, but rather a
reproach which must be brought against reason as such, that it
cannot make comprehensible the absolute necessity of an unconditioned practical law (such as the categorical imperative must
be). For its unwillingness to do this by means of a condition—
namely, by basing this necessity on some underlying interest—
reason cannot be blamed, since in that case there would be no
moral law, that is, no supreme law of freedom. And thus, while
we do not comprehend the practical unconditioned necessity of
the moral imperative, we do comprehend its *incomprehensibility*.
This is all that can fairly be asked of a philosophy which presses
forward in its principles to the very limit of human reason.

NOTES

(The first figure given is the page number of the second German edition, as shown in the margin of the translation. The cross-references also refer to these pages.)

PREFACE

ii, n. 1. There can, however, be an applied logic; *see* p. 32 footnote.

v, n. 1. That is, a metaphysic of morals.

vi, n. 1. Anthropology is roughly equivalent to what we should now call psychology, though the latter title is usually reserved by Kant for theories about the soul as an incorporeal substance.

vi, n. 2. 'Idea'—with a capital I—is a technical term for a concept of the unconditioned (especially of an unconditioned totality or whole), and on Kant's view duty is unconditioned (or absolute). On the other hand, 'idea'—with a small i—is used in the ordinary English sense: it is a translation of the German *Vorstellung*. For 'Idea' *see* also the analysis of pp. 127-28. We find 'Idea' used also more loosely, as on page x, for the concept of an organic whole—e.g. a science.

vi, n. 3. Kant seems to have in mind such a precept as 'Honesty is the best policy'. This commends the universal duty of honesty by an appeal to the empirical motive of self-interest.

vii, n. 1. But *see* also p. 35. It is only the ultimate principles that require no anthropology.

vii, n. 2. Inclinations are for Kant *habitual* desires.

viii, n. 1. That is, a metaphysic of morals—not of nature.

ix, n. 1. This work by Christian Wolff was published in 1738-39.

x, n. 1. Kant has in mind his own Transcendental Logic (as set forth in the *Critique of Pure Reason*)—the logic of pure *a priori* knowledge, not of all thinking as such.

xi, n. 1. Metaphysics is here the metaphysic of nature.

xii, n. 1. That is to say, it is liable to fall into contradictions (antinomies) and illusions.

CHAPTER I

2, n. 1. This sentence should be noted as it affirms what Kant is commonly supposed to deny.

2, n. 2. That is, these qualities are not good when they are incompatible with a good will.

2, n. 3. An affection (*Affekt*) is a sudden passion like anger and is compared by Kant to intoxication. A passion (*Leidenschaft*) is a lasting passion or obsession like hate and is compared by Kant to a disease.

6, n. 1. The use of the word 'misology' is one of the passages which show the influence of Plato's *Phaedo* on Kant's ethical theory. This was due to the publication in 1767 of Moses Mendelssohn's *Phädon*—a work which is in great part a translation of Plato.

7, n. 1. Kant never claims—as it is too commonly said—that a good will is the sole good.

7, n. 2. Observe Kant's recognition of the 'contentment' found in good action. The view that he regarded this—or even a more mundane satisfaction —as diminishing or destroying the goodness of an action is a pure fabrication.

8, n. 1. Kant's view is always that obstacles make a good will more *conspicuous*—not that a good will is shown only in overcoming obstacles.

9, n. 1. The example refers, not to the preceding sentence, but to the one before that. It is not so easy as Kant suggests to distinguish between actions done from duty and actions done from self-interest—even a grocer may have a conscience. Nevertheless he is right in saying that an action done solely out of self-interest is not commonly regarded as morally good.

9, n. 2. For 'maxim' *see* the footnotes to pp. 15 and 51.

10, n. 1. Strictly speaking, it stands on the same footing as an *action* done from such inclinations as the inclination for honour.

12, n. 1. Happiness, as is indicated immediately below, is the *satisfaction* of all inclinations as a sum.

13, n. 1. It should be noted that Kant has neglected—presumably by an oversight—to state his *first* proposition in a *general* form.

13, n. 2. That is, as Kant indicates below, the controlling maxim must be formal, not material, where an action is done for the sake of duty.

16, footnote, n. 1. Strictly speaking, it is reverence (and not the law) which is analogous to fear and inclination.

17, footnote, n. 1. *See* pp. 55–56.

19, n. 1. This looks like falling back on mere self-interest, but Kant's point is that there could be *no promises at all* if this maxim were universally followed. *See* p. 18 above, also pp. 55 and 49.

20, n. 1. The highest grades of knowledge are for Kant 'insight' and (above insight) 'comprehension.' *See* pp. 120 and 123, and also *K.M.E.*, I 334.

CHAPTER II

28, n. 1. It should be noted that it is contained as *duty in general*—not as a specific duty.

28, n. 2. This need not mean that one rule cannot over-ride another.

29, n. 1. This whole passage again suggests the influence of Plato. For the special point about the concept of God *see* p. 92.

31, n. 1. Metaphysics is here a metaphysic of morals.

33, n. 1. Dignity is a technical term for intrinsic value. *See* p. 77.

33, footnote, n. 1. Professor J. G. Sulzer (1720–79) translated Hume's *Enquiry* into German in 1755.

34, n. 1. Here again Kant is warning us only against contaminating moral *principles* by the addition of non-moral motives. To do this is to diminish the value of corresponding actions, as when we advocate honesty on the ground that it is the best policy.

35, n. 1. Speculative or theoretical philosophy has to allow, not only that human reason is discursive (in the sense that its concepts give us no knowledge apart from sensuous intuition), but also that for knowledge it is dependent on pure intuitions of space and time, which may be *peculiar* to human beings.

35, n. 2. We cannot, however, derive moral principles by mere *analysis* of the concept 'rational being'; *see* p. 50, footnote. For such derivation we require a *synthetic* use of reason; *see* p. 96.

35, n. 3. Metaphysics is here a metaphysic of morals.

36, n. 1. In Chapter I.

36, n. 2. Ideas in a metaphysic of morals (as elsewhere) go to a 'complete totality' such as can never be given in experience.

36, n. 3. We must pass from subjective principles (or maxims) to conditioned objective principles (hypothetical imperatives), and from them to the unconditioned categorical imperative of duty (especially the imperative of autonomy—pp. 69 ff.—which prepares the way for the concept of freedom). This can be clear only on a second reading.

36, n. 4. If this 'derivation' were logical deduction, we could hardly infer from it that the will is practical reason. Kant seems to have in mind something more like what Aristotle called a *practical* syllogism—one whose conclusion is not a proposition, but an action.

37, n. 1. 'Determined' here means '*objectively* determined'—not '*subjectively* determined' as it means in a later sentence on this page.

38, footnote, n. 1. Such a rule is a hypothetical imperative.

40, n. 1. The word 'its' refers to the will.

41, n. 1. The edition of the Berlin Academy strikes out the German word equivalent to 'not'.

42, n. 1. Prudence might perhaps better be described as rational self-love.

42, footnote, n. 1. This is one of the places where Kant indicates that prudence is concerned, not merely with means, but with the harmonization of ends.

44, n. 1. To be practically necessary is to be objectively necessary; compare page 50 footnote. To be theoretically necessary would be to fall under the necessity of nature, which is something quite different. *See* p. 97.

44, n. 2. This will become clearer in Chapter III.

44, n. 3. That is to say, we are concerned, not with finding out the means necessary to an end, but with the obligation to use these means when they are known.

44, footnote, n. 1. A pragmatic sanction is an imperial or royal decree having the effect of a fundamental law. Examples are the edict of Charles VII of France in 1438—the basis of the liberties of the Gallican church; and that of the Emperor Charles VI in 1724 determining the Austrian succession. Kant considers such sanctions to be prudential—not as following from the system of natural law which applies to all States as such.

45, n. 1. We are dealing—as Kant indicates in the next clause—with the *concept* of willing an end. In analytic propositions we have to distinguish sharply between the *concept* of the subject and the subject itself (usually a thing and not a concept).

49, n. 1. We have to show, not only *how* a categorical imperative is possible, but also *that* it is possible.

50, footnote, n. 1. The willing of an action enjoined by a categorical imperative cannot be derived by analysing the concept of willing an end (as is done in the case of a hypothetical imperative).

50, footnote, n. 2. We shall, however, find in Chapter III—*see* especially pp. 111-12—that the *Idea* of such a perfect will is necessary in order to establish the synthetic *a priori* practical propositions of morality.

50, footnote, n. 3. To say that the categorical imperative connects an action *immediately* with the concept of a rational will is to say that the connexion is not derived from the presupposed willing of some further end. Yet in spite of this *immediate* connexion the proposition remains synthetic: the willing of the action is *not* contained in the concept of a rational will.

51, n. 1. The maxim in question is a *material* maxim. *See T.C.I.*, pp. 135-6.

51, footnote, n. 1. An objective principle is an imperative only for finite agents who are imperfectly rational.

52, n. 1. The use of a preposition here (and elsewhere) may seem an unnecessary complication. Perhaps Kant wishes to emphasize the *interpenetration* of the material and formal maxim. In willing in accordance with a material maxim I will *at the same time* that this maxim should be a universal law. As a material maxim is based on sensuous motives, this formula by itself disposes of the traditional doctrine that in a morally good action a sensuous motive can never, on Kant's view, be present at the same time as the moral motive.

52, n. 2. When we speak of 'nature', we may take it in a *material* sense as equivalent to the sum total of *phenomena*; or we may take it in a *formal* sense as equivalent to the sum total of the *laws* governing the existence of natural phenomena. This second usage is more akin to popular phrases like 'the nature of man' and 'the nature of the world'. Hence we might say, speaking popularly, that it is the nature of the world to be governed by the law of cause and effect. In spite of this, Kant treats the laws of nature as purposive when he asks if our maxims can be conceived or willed as laws of nature. *See* also pp. 81, 84, and 80, footnote.

53, footnote, n. 1. *See* my analysis of the argument. In *T.C.I.*, pp. 147-8, I laid too much stress on the over-riding of one duty by another. The main point is the 'latitude' allowed to inclination in imperfect duties.

53, footnote, n. 2. Outer duties are duties to others; inner duties are duties to myself.

54, n. 1. Many commentators say that Kant condemns suicide on the ground that if everyone committed suicide there would be no one left to do so! There is clearly no trace of such an argument here (or indeed anywhere else, so far as I know), and the reader should be on his guard against such absurdities.

56, n. 1. This is put in a prudential way, but Kant's doctrine is not prudential, as can be seen from p. 11 and p. 68, footnote.

57, n. 1. This distinction is the same as that between perfect and imperfect duties.

57, n. 2. Kant is dealing only with the four main types of duty (perfect and imperfect, inner and outer). Every type has different kinds of obligation falling under it according as it is concerned with different kinds of object. For example, perfect duties to others include duties not to assail their freedom or steal their property, as well as not to borrow on false pretences. *See* p. 68.

60, n. 1. Kant is again dealing with degrees of conspicuousness, not with degrees of excellence. *See* n. 1. on p. 8.

61, n. 1. The point is that we must not introduce empirical considerations into the *principle of morality*. The moral principle must by itself be sufficient to determine action, but this does not mean that other motives may not be present *at the same time*.

61, n. 2. By embracing a cloud in mistake for Juno Ixion became the father of the 'mongrel' race of centaurs.

62, n. 1. The proposition establishing this *a priori* connexion is, however, not analytic but synthetic. *See* p. 50, footnote.

62, n. 2. Here a metaphysic of morals is taken to include a critique of practical reason. The latter is specially concerned with *justifying* the *a priori* connexion between the moral law and a rational will as such. *See* pp. 87 and 95–96.

62, n. 3. These differences—between the pleasant, the beautiful, and the good—are discussed in the *Critique of Judgement*, e.g. in §. 5.

63, n. 1. As we have seen (pp. i–iii), physics (or natural philosophy) must have an empirical, as well as an *a priori*, part. This empirical part is in turn divided into two parts, the first of which is concerned with the world of physical nature, while the second (which is here in question) is concerned with mind.

63, n. 2. I have here ventured—perhaps rashly—to substitute 'subjective' for 'objective'. 'An objective ground'—if it could mean anything here— would have to mean 'a ground in objects'. This sense is very rare in Kant and would be most confusing in a passage where everywhere else 'objective' means valid for every rational being as such. On the other hand Kant always emphasizes that ends (whether objective or subjective) must be subjectively chosen—we can never be compelled to make anything our end. *See*, for example, the use of the word 'subjectively' on p. 70, especially the second use of it. Every end is a subjective ground of the will's self-determination. If it is given solely by reason, it becomes an objective ground as well.

63, n. 3. A means considered as the ground (or cause) of the possibility of an action seems to be an instrument. Thus, for example, a hammer is (or contains) the ground of the possibility of knocking in a nail. In practice, however, Kant usually treats an action itself as a means (the means enjoined by a hypothetical imperative).

64, n. 1. Compare p. 14.

64, n. 2. If Kant means 'every volition' strictly, he must have in mind universal *principles* only—not particular moral laws.

65, n. 1. We might expect inclinations to be grounded on needs, but Kant appears usually to take the view that needs are grounded on inclinations.

65, n. 2. Kant is not usually so hostile to inclinations. Is his attitude here perhaps due to the influence of the *Phaedo*?

66, n. 1. Here Kant distinguishes clearly between a supreme practical *principle* valid for all rational beings as such and a corresponding categorical *imperative* valid for imperfectly rational agents such as men. This distinction should always be kept in mind where it is not made explicitly.

66, n. 2. Strictly speaking, 'humanity' should be 'rational nature as such', but the only rational nature with which we are acquainted is to be found in man. Kant himself makes this distinction at the beginning of the previous paragraph.

66, n. 3. The word 'simply' is essential to Kant's meaning since we all have to use other men as means.

66, footnote, n. 1. The reference is to pp. 99–100 and 101–02. A rational being can act only under the Idea of freedom, and so must conceive himself as autonomous and therefore as an end in himself.

68, footnote, n. 1. 'Don't do to others what you don't want done to yourself.'

68, footnote, n. 2. It should be observed that here Kant regards a law as universal only if it covers *all* duties and so is an ultimate principle. So far as he uses 'universal law' in this sense, his claim that it is independent of knowledge of human nature is at least not palpably absurd.

69, n. 1. The *purpose* (or *end*) *of nature* for humanity is to be sharply distinguished from the *natural purpose* (or *end*) which all men seek (as in the paragraph immediately following). The first conception supposes nature to have a final end or aim which is not to be found in nature itself. The second rests on observation of nature and can be confirmed by such observation. See *Critique of Judgement*, §. 67.

71, n. 1. Here Kant is not bidding us to renounce all interests: we have, for example, a right, and even an indirect duty, to seek our own happiness. What he is saying is that the categorical imperative cannot be based on any interest: it excludes from its *sovereign authority* 'every admixture of interest as a motive'. Our judgement of duty must in no way be influenced by our interests—this is the only sense in which all interests must be renounced.

72, n. 1. Kant is considering the hypothesis that we are bound to obey moral laws only because of self-interest. He argues that a will bound by self-interest would not always issue in right actions unless it was bound by a *further* law bidding it act on maxims of self-interest *only* when these maxims were capable of being willed as universal laws; *see* also p. 94. Hence a will bound by self-interest could not be a *supreme* law-giver nor would it make *universal* law.

73, n. 1. Although Kant says 'natural purpose' (*Naturzweck*), he must mean 'purpose of nature' (*Zweck der Natur*). *See* n. 1 on p. 69 above.

74, n. 1. Here we are not considering the *content* of personal ends (which has just been excluded). What we are considering is only the *form* of a kingdom of ends composed of persons capable of willing personal ends (whatever be their content) *in conformity with universal law*.

75, n. 1. Could this mean, that unlike us, God as omnipotent is not thwarted by the will of others? Or that He is not subject to State law? Or that as holy He is not under the categorical imperative considered as a divine command?

77, n. 1. This is a reference to Kant's own aesthetic theory. I use the term 'fancy price' (in the absence of a better) to mean a value for fancy or imagination.

78, n. 1. It may seem a moralistic prejudice on Kant's part thus to put moral value so far above aesthetic value. Yet when we consider what we think of men who combine the finest aesthetic taste with fiendish cruelty (as happened in some cases during the war), we may begin to incline towards Kant's view.

80, n. 1. A complete determination combines both form and matter.

80, n. 2. Unity, multiplicity (or plurality), and totality are the three categories of *quantity*, the last of which combines the other two.

81, n. 1. It would be a more natural rendering to say 'bring the *action* nearer to intuition'. But an action is already near to intuition, and what we require to bring nearer to intuition is the universal formula (or the Idea of reason, as on pp. 79–80 above).

81, n. 2. *See* also n. 2. on p. 52.

81, n. 3. It is not clear whether 'object' means object of thought or object (purpose) of will. On p. 98 'object' is apparently equated with 'content', but this again is ambiguous.

82, n. 1. Kant forgets that in the case of imperfect (or wider) duties the end in itself is conceived positively.

84, n. 1. Rational beings are here regarded as the *ends (or purposes) of nature*. *See* n. 1 on p. 69. This teleological assumption is also made in Kant's use of the universal law of nature as an analogy for the universal law of morality (or freedom).

84, n. 2. The introduction of happiness as a reward for virtue is a trifle crude. It would be more satisfactory to say, as Kant does elsewhere, that without the co-operation of nature the good will could not be successful in realizing its ends.

86, n. 1. The reference is to pp. 14 ff., especially to the footnote on pp. 16–17.

88, n. 1. Analysis of concepts seems here to produce synthetic propositions. Does Kant refer to an analytic argument? *See* my analysis of p. xiv.

89, n. 1. This is not the inhuman doctrine that a good man should not be influenced by any desire for objects, but that he should not allow his desire for any object to interfere with his judgement of duty.

89, n. 2. Kant is referring to the reason which is the basis of the categorical imperative. This reason cannot be merely that I happen to be interested in the happiness of others.

91, footnote, n. 1. Francis Hutcheson (1694–1747), Professor of Moral Philosophy in the University of Glasgow, was the leading exponent of the doctrine of moral sense. Kant was himself for some time influenced by this doctrine.

92, n. 1. Kant has in mind the doctrines of Christian Wolff (1679–1754) and his followers. *See* n. 1. on p. ix.

92, n. 2. The reference is primarily to the doctrine of Crusius (1712–76).

92, n. 3. The reference is to the *ontological* concept of perfection mentioned above.

94, n. 1. If any object of will is made the basis for morality, we require (1) a law binding us to pursue this object, and (2)—if the law is to issue always in right actions—a *further* law bidding us act on the maxim of pursuing this object *only* when the maxim is capable of being willed as a universal law. *See* n. 1. on p. 72.

96, n. 1. This passage (together with p. xiv) suggests a connexion between a synthetic argument and synthetic propositions. I do not see how this can be so since the same propositions must appear in both analytic and synthetic arguments. *See* my analysis of the argument of p. xiv and also my note on p. 88.

CHAPTER III

98, n. 1. *See* n. 3. on p. 81.

98, n. 2. A will 'under moral laws' is not a will which always acts according to moral laws, but one which would so act if reason had full control over passion. See *Critique of Judgement*, §. 87 (the long footnote). Even a bad will is under moral laws and is free.

99, n. 1. The two 'cognitions' may be thought of as the subject and the predicate of a synthetic proposition so long as we have in mind only categorical propositions; but we must remember that hypothetical and disjunctive propositions may also be synthetic.

99, n. 2. The Idea in question is made more precise in pp. 111–12, where it is the Idea of my will as belonging to the intelligible world and as active on its own account—that is, as free.

100, n. 1. This parenthesis is obscure in the German text, and, strictly speaking, it is not possible to demonstrate freedom *a priori*: all we can show *a priori* is that a rational agent must necessarily act on the presupposition of freedom.

100, footnote, n. 1. The burden which weighs upon theory is the burden of a task which cannot be carried out: it is impossible to prove freedom theoretically, though we can show from a theoretical point of view that freedom is not incompatible with natural necessity.

101, n. 1. It should be observed that Kant appeals first to *theoretical* reason as a power of judgement.

101, n. 2. It is not clear whether this is merely an inference or whether practical reason has the same insight into its own presuppositions as has theoretical reason.

102, n. 1. *See* n. 1 on p. 66, footnote.

102, n. 2. The German text has 'Ideas' in the plural, but this seems to be a slip.

103, n. 1. Compare pp. 37 and 39.

104, n. 1. 'States' here may cover agreeable 'states of affairs' as well as 'states of feeling'.

105, n. 1. Reciprocal concepts are concepts which have the same denotation (that is, which apply to precisely the same objects). Thus, for example the concept of a three-sided rectilineal figure and the concept of a three-angled rectilineal figure are reciprocal concepts.

106, n. 1. Inner sensation or inner sense may be identified with what is sometimes called 'introspection'.

107, n. 1. A subject here is a subject known—through inner sense—as an *object* of experience.

107, n. 2. Not only as an object of inner sense, but also *as a subject capable of sensing* (and so as an object affected through the senses—p. 117), I must regard myself as belonging to the world of sense.

107, n. 3. To manifest pure activity is to think and act on principles of reason. We know these principles (and so far this activity) immediately—i.e. not through sense.

108, n. 1. Reason is here used in a technical sense as a power of *Ideas*, while understanding is a power of *categories*.

108, n. 2. To mark out the limits of the sensible world is to mark out the limits of understanding; for apart from sensibility understanding can think nothing at all.

109, n. 1. This does not mean that men always act morally, but that they act on the presupposition of freedom and so of a moral law to which they are subject.

111, n. 1. 'Immediately' means independently of sensuous impulsions and their objects.

111, n. 2. That is, a ground of actions and laws in the sensible world. My new version here was suggested by a criticism of Dr. Dieter Henrich (*Philosophische Rundschau*, 2. Jahrgang, Heft 1/2, 35 a.). The discussion in the first two editions of *T.C.I.* was based on a common mistranslation; but the present version confirms its conclusion. For a fuller discussion see the Appendix to Chapter XXIV of the third edition of *T.C.I.*, pp. 250-2.

111, n. 3. *See* n. 2 on p. 99.

114, n. 1. That is, as objectively (not subjectively) necessary. *See* p. 37.

114, n. 2. For dialectic *see* pp. 23-24 and my note on p. xii.

116, n. 1. '*Bonum vacans*' is unoccupied property.

118, n. 1. The extent of this 'knowledge' is considerably curtailed in the following paragraph.

118, n. 2. *See* n. 1 on p. 111—a passage with which the present statement should be compared.

119, n. 1. To say that the *concept* of the intelligible world is only a point of view is *not* to say that the intelligible world itself is only a point of view; and we must remember that the concept of the sensible world can with equal justification be described as a point of view.

120, n. 1. Observe the distinction between 'comprehension' and 'insight'. To comprehend—*see* p. 123—is to make intelligible *a priori*. *See* also n. 1 on p. 20.

122, n. 1. Compare n. 2 on p. 7.

124, n. 1. That is, *as far as reason is concerned*. *See* pp. 111-12.

125, n. 1. The reference is presumably to natural philosophy or physics in Kant's wide sense.

INDEX OF PROPER NAMES
AND GENERAL INDEX

The page numbers in both these indices refer to the smaller numbers given in the margin of the translation. These correspond to the numbers of the pages in the second edition of the original.

INDEX OF PROPER NAMES

GENERAL INDEX